THOREAU AS SPIRITUAL GUIDE

THOREAU AS SPIRITUAL GUIDE

A COMPANION TO

Walden

FOR PERSONAL REFLECTION
AND GROUP DISCUSSION

BARRY M. ANDREWS

SKINNER HOUSE BOOKS
Boston

Published by Skinner House Books. Skinner House Books is an imprint of the Unitarian Universalist Association, a liberal religious organization with more than 1,000 congregations in the U.S. and Canada. 25 Beacon Street, Boston, MA 02108-2800.

Printed in Canada

ISBN 1-55896-405-3

04 03 02 01
10 9 8 7 6 5 4 3 2

Cover illustration by Patricia Frevert
Text design by Terry Bain

NOTE: An edition of *Walden* with an introduction and annotations by social and environmental critic Bill McKibben (1997) is available from Beacon Press.

All quotations are from *Walden* unless otherwise specified.

To Linda,
my loving wife and spiritual companion,
for her unfailing encouragement and support.

CONTENTS

There is a deep longing within many people today for something more, something different, something better. At some level, I think we can all agree that we would like to have more beauty in our lives, more of nature in our cities, more time for contemplation, more of an opportunity to enjoy life in all of its fullness and vitality. Partly out of inertia, partly out of fear of change and partly out of not knowing how to begin or which way to go, we have a hard time making a commitment to what Thomas Moore calls "the care of the soul." This is not easy. The cultivation of the soul requires a certain amount of discipline. Soul work also has a tendency to reveal discrepancies between our aspirations and the everyday realities we face. It confronts us with the need to make choices about how we will live our lives. But, I must say, it can also be an exciting voyage of self-discovery, and, in any event, it is the only way to true happiness.

To quote the philosopher Epicurus, "it is never too early or too late to care for the well-being of the soul." Whether or not they fully realize it, people today are complaining about the lack of soul or depth in their lives. As a minister, people often remark to me that they are experiencing a certain emptiness or sense of meaninglessness; that they are vaguely depressed and disillusioned about commitments and relationships, and that they feel a yearning for personal fulfillment and spiritual growth. These concerns are a reflection of the hunger for spirituality that has brought so many people to our congregations in the past few years. It also accounts for the popularity of so many of our adult education classes—at least those that deal with issues in relation to spiritual growth. I have heard many people comment that the rewards society has to offer, including, money, power, sex, entertainment and material goods, are ultimately distractions and positive hindrances to living a more meaningful, fulfilling and spiritual life.

There is generally a feeling that we are overworked and undernourished. Life is lived at such a frenetic pace that much of what we do—from work to parenting to play—seems inadequate and superficial. Our much-heralded technological innovations, including e-mail and the Internet, seem, in Thoreau's view of such things, to be improved means to as yet unimproved ends. We sense a lack of depth and intimacy in our relationships. And because we have confused stimulation with fulfillment, nothing ever quite measures up to our expectations. In spite of Unitarian Universalists' customary aversion to religious language, more and more of us are agreed that these are essentially spiritual issues, and have contributed to the clogging of the arteries of the soul.

Increasingly, Unitarian Universalists are looking for answers to the problems of contemporary living, and, in doing so have turned to many of the traditional sources of spiritual wisdom and strength, including prayer, meditation, healing, dream work, religious retreats, and the like. Nor is this simply an interest shared by those new to our congregations. Many long-time Unitarian Universalists—dyed-in-the-wool humanists among them—are also engaging in fundamental aspects of soul work. I think these developments are healthy, not only for us personally, but also for Unitarian Universalism. For too long, we've been viewed—and even seen ourselves—as an alternative to religion rather than as a religious alternative, which is what we truly are.

I don't mean to suggest that this burgeoning interest in spirituality is something that's happened over night. In fact, it has been going on for quite some time. For as long as I have been an active Unitarian Universalist, a period of some thirty years now, there have been those who have had a more than passing interest in Eastern philosophies, including Hinduism, Buddhism and Taoism. More recently, Unitarian Universalists have been actively involved in such pursuits as Transcendental Meditation, yoga and tai chi, feminist spirituality, Native American religions, and numerous other forms of spirituality.

I myself have been a student of Eastern religions, Taoism in particular, for many years. I am a sometime practitioner of tai-chi and meditation. I have a keen interest in Native American spirituality, and was once initiated as a Crow medicine person. I have attended dozens of retreats, conferences, seminars and workshops on these and other religious traditions and practices. I suspect many of you could say the same. Nevertheless, for all of these involvements, I do not consider myself a Taoist or a Native American shaman. I am a card-carrying Unitarian Universalist, deeply committed to our own principles and practices.

It is part of the genius of our movement to be inclusive of persons of different religious backgrounds and to be open to the wisdom of other spiritual traditions. Even the Transcendentalists were avid readers of the religious scriptures of the Near and Far East. We grow and Unitarian Universalism progresses (if I may use that much maligned word) through exposure to other religious ways of life. But the fact of the matter is that other religious philosophies and disciplines are not everyone's cup of tea. While traditional, they are not necessarily mainstream. They are a little too exotic for some tastes. And, especially where native religions are concerned, it is difficult if not impossible to get past the problems associated with cultural differences. Still, our interest in these matters is indicative of the serious desire many Unitarian Universalists have to cultivate the soul and deepen their spiritual lives. It also attests to the need for models perhaps closer to hand and more philosophically and temperamentally akin to us.

I do not for a moment wish to take anything away from those who have found wisdom in other traditions nor to diminish the importance of what other religions have to offer. As I suggested before, I think we are enriched by the exposure to different forms of spirituality. But I also believe that, unbeknownst to many, we are the inheritors of a deeply and profoundly spiritual tradition of our own. What is more, this tradition is not only uniquely Unitarian Universalist, but also typically American, and offers us a valuable model for the cultivation of the soul.

Unitarian Universalist scholar David Robinson has remarked, "Like a pauper who searches for the next meal, never knowing of the relatives whose will would make him rich, American Unitarians lament their vague religious identity, standing upon the richest spiritual legacy of any American denomination. Possessed of a deep and sustaining history of spiritual achievement and philosophical speculation, religious liberals have been, ironically, dispossessed of that heritage." He observes that Unitarian Universalists suffer from a disturbing malaise. On the one hand, we seem troubled by a vague sense of our religious identity and our marginal place among the established American faiths. On the other hand, he notes that Unitarian Universalists, like many other Americans, are searching for a greater sense of spirituality in their lives and churches. Both of these conditions are linked in Robinson's mind with a collective amnesia or ignorance concerning our own very rich and compelling spiritual heritage.

The heritage of which Robinson speaks is, of course, that of American Transcendentalism. It is important to understand, first of all, that Transcendentalism was essentially a religious movement; in particular, it was an outgrowth of early nineteenth century Unitarianism. Virtually all of the Transcendentalists were Unitarians, and most of them were ministers. Some, like Ralph Waldo Emerson, left the ministry for a wider audience; others, like Theodore Parker, continued to preach Transcendentalism from their pulpits. The Transcendentalists were responsible for much of the literature and many of the reforms in American culture and society in the decades leading up to the Civil War. But in all they said and did, the cultivation of the soul was their foremost concern.

They experienced at first hand the changes wrought by the transition from an agrarian to an industrial society. They witnessed the advance of technology and the rise of consumerism. Their writings were a direct response to the conditions of life in their day—and at the dawning of our own era. Indeed the issues were heightened for them because of the contrast between the life-styles of the farm and factory. Today, we have difficulty imagining a different way of life from the one we have become so accustomed to. The Transcendentalists were troubled by many of the changes they saw. Yet they drew upon an enormous reserve of spiritual resources to help reshape the image of American society. Beginning with the fundamental notion of what they termed "self-culture," they experimented with a multitude of spiritual paths and practices, taking them into hitherto uncharted territories of personal self-expression and social reform.

More than anything else, the Transcendentalists tried to achieve a balance in their lives between work and leisure, nature and civilization, society and solitude, spiritual aspirations and moral behavior. They did so on the basis of a this-worldly form of spirituality characterized by a reverence for nature, an organic world-view, a sense of the miraculous, an optimism about human potential, a search for what is universal in religion and personal experience, a strong ethical sensibility, and an encouragement of the individual in his or her own religious quest.

Even though they referred to it as "the newness," the Transcendentalists understood that the spirituality they espoused was, in actuality, a form of what Aldous Huxley, among others, termed the perennial philosophy. In his own essay on Transcendentalism, Emerson noted that the so-called "new views" "are not new, but they are the very oldest of thoughts cast into the mould of these new times." The light is everywhere and always the same, but is revealed to us by what it falls upon. The light itself is transparent and formless. In the same way, the soul is revealed in the teachings of this new form of universal wisdom. In Emerson's words, the Transcendentalist "adopts the whole connection of spiritual doctrine. He believes in miracle, in the perpetual openness of the human mind to a new influx of light and power; he believes in inspiration and ecstasy."

And so, none of what I will be telling you will be new—not that Transcendentalism is a new form of spirituality for us, nor even that it was so for the Transcendentalists themselves. But it is perhaps new for us in the same way it was for them, namely, a new occasion for an influx of light and power in our own lives. My own spiritual life has been significantly enriched by the insights of the Transcendentalists. I would like to explore some of these insights with you, not so much in the guise of a guru, but more as an interpreter or guide. The Transcendentalists themselves are not always transparent and many of their key ideas will need translating.

Historians frequently date the Transcendentalist movement from the 1830s to the end of the Civil War. Fundamentally, however, Transcendentalism did not die out with the passing of the likes of Emerson, Thoreau, Parker and Margaret Fuller, but in fact became one of the major currents in the development of Unitarian Universalism. As it entered the theological mainstream in the later decades of the nineteenth century, fewer and fewer Unitarians were avowed Transcendentalists. Proud to claim Emerson, Parker, Fuller and the others, we have remained relatively unaware of the historical connection between Unitarianism and Transcendentalism and have to a large extent neglected our unique spiritual heritage. But to paraphrase Epicurus, I would insist that it is never too soon or too late to reclaim it.

SELF-CULTURE

Transcendentalism and the Care of the Soul

ⓖ

In spite of its widespread ramifications in American culture and society, Transcendentalism was at the core a religious movement. This is true not only because of its origins as a theological revolt within the ranks of Unitarianism, but also because, in every area, including literature, education and politics, its initial impulse and primary purpose was essentially spiritual in nature.

The Transcendentalists themselves had been inspired by the preaching of William Ellery Channing. Channing was the major proponent of Unitarianism as it broke away from Calvinism in the previous generation. Channing was a deeply spiritual figure who inspired and even supported the Transcendentalists. Emerson referred to him as "our Bishop" and "the star of the American Church." In particular, the Transcendentalists seized and built upon the notion of "self-culture" which Channing had articulated so convincingly in his sermons. This notion held that the goal of the religious life was the culture or cultivation of one's inner spiritual nature, or soul. Here is how he describes it in an address entitled "Self-Culture":

> To cultivate any thing, be it a plant, an animal, a mind, is to make grow. Growth, expansion, is the end. Nothing admits culture but that which has a principle of life, capable of being expanded. He, therefore, who does what he can to unfold all his powers and capacities, especially his nobler ones, so as to become a well-proportioned, vigorous, happy being, practices self-culture.

1

Quite apart from the way the word is understood today, culture in Channing's time still had primarily agricultural associations, in keeping with an agrarian economy and outlook. And, in contrast to the more narrowly psychological concept of the self we have now, self was then essentially equated with one's spirit or soul. Quite simply, self-culture meant spiritual growth or cultivation of the soul. Self-culture introduced a developmental or progressive view of the spiritual life, replacing the notion of conversion as a single, decisive event with that of religious growth as an on-going process. However, just as the potential for spiritual development is limitless, a concerted effort at spiritual discipline is necessary to achieve it. What is more, this self-discipline required that inward aspirations be manifested in outward ethical behavior. In other words, introspection was necessarily wedded to social action.

It was Channing's emphasis on the spiritual capacity of the soul and the importance of cultivating the seed of divinity within each individual that had tremendous appeal to the Transcendentalists. Virtually all of them were engaged in one way or another with the pursuit of self-culture, and it accounted for everything from methods of spiritual discipline to experiments with alternate life-styles and efforts at social and religious reform. As Margaret Fuller noted in her Memoirs: "Very early on I knew that the only object in life was to grow. I was often false to this knowledge, in idolatries of particular objects, or impatient longings for happiness, but I have never lost sight of it, have always been controlled by it, and this first gift of love has never been superceded by a later [one]."

The gospel of self-culture was at the heart of Emerson's philosophy as well. In an early series of lectures on "Human Culture" he maintained that one's "own culture, the unfolding of his own nature, is the chief end of man. A divine impulse at the core of his being impels him to this." According to Emerson, the self or soul did not need to be cultivated in keeping with criteria external to the soul itself, but simply encouraged to develop spontaneously, according to the promptings of its own nature. Self-culture for Emerson, as for the Transcendentalists generally, was a natural development of the spirit in response to which what is required is "to remove all obstructions and let this natural force have free play."

What Emerson and others found missing from first-generation Unitarianism was this emphasis on the soul. Of course, Channing encouraged it; but it was left to the Transcendentalists to develop it and apply it to virtually every sphere of human activity. Theodore Parker, one of those who remained in the Unitarian ministry in spite of efforts to drive him out, expressed his dissatisfaction with "orthodox" Unitarianism in his own memoirs:

> I felt early that the liberal ministers did not do justice to simple religious feeling; to all their preaching seemed to relate too much to outward things, not enough to the inward pious life.... Most powerfully preaching to the Understanding, the Conscience and the Will, the cry was ever, "Duty, Duty! Work, Work!" They failed to address with equal power, the Soul, and did not also shout "Joy, Joy! Delight, Delight!"

"Pale negations," "corpse-cold," "lifeless," added Emerson to a growing chorus of complaints among the Transcendentalist Unitarians.

The term, "transcendentalism," itself was derived from the writings of Emmanuel Kant, a German philosopher, whose ideas influenced the English Romantics and were now popular among those espousing the New Views. As Parker explained it, there were two schools of philosophy, the sensational philosophy of John Locke (and the "orthodox" Unitarians), which held that there was nothing in the intellect that was not first in the senses; the other, the intuitive philosophy attributed to Kant which held, in Parker's words, that we have "faculties which transcend the senses; faculties which give [us] ideas and intuitions that transcend sensational experience.... This is the transcendental school." According to Parker, the deepest religious and moral truths—the existence and nature of God, the difference between right and wrong—could not be demonstrated empirically. They could only be known intuitively, by faculties that transcend the senses. Hence the term transcendentalism.

The Transcendentalists also distinguished between the two schools in terms of a distinction between Reason and the Understanding—meaning by these terms pretty much the opposite of what they signify today. For them, Reason was an intuitive faculty; Understanding a rational, intellectual process. As Emerson described them,

Reason is the highest faculty of the soul, what we mean by the soul itself; it never reasons, never proves; it simply perceives, it is vision. The Understanding toils all the time, compares, contrives, adds, argues; near-sighted, dwelling in the present, the expedient, the customary.

Emerson identified the Understanding with the intellect and Reason with what he termed the religious or moral sensibility, and argued that it is through this indwelling sentiment, intuitively, that we have access to the realm of the spirit.

It would be going too far, I think, to suggest that the Transcendentalists were mystics, and yet there is a strong mystical strain in all their writing. Theirs, after all, was a religion of insight and not of tradition. And, in light of the distinction they made between Reason and Understanding, it is not surprising that religious truth was revealed to them in moments of mystical awareness. This was perhaps most pronounced in Emerson, but it was characteristic of the other Transcendentalists as well. Margaret Fuller, for example, describes such a moment in her Memoirs. She had been despondent, feeling that the world had no place for her and that the church did not offer any spiritual comfort. Pausing beside a stream at the end of a long walk through the countryside on a bleak day, she had an experience which she describes in this way:

I saw there was no self; that selfishness was all folly, and the result of circumstance; that it was only because I thought the self real that I suffered; that I had only to live in the idea of the all, and all was mine. This truth came to me, and I received it unhesitatingly; so that I was for that hour taken up to God. In that true ray most of the relations of earth seemed mere films, phenomena.

These moments gave rise to what Emerson called "double consciousness," a heightening of the contradiction between Reason and the Understanding:

... one prevails now, all buzz and din; and the other prevails then, all infinitude and paradise; and, with the progress of life, the two discover no greater disposition to reconcile themselves.... [Y]et we retain the belief that this petty web we weave will at last be overshot and reticulated with veins of the blue, and that the moments will characterize the days.

This is an awareness that mystical states are transitory, and yet of such intensity and value that the rest of our life seems shallow and superficial by comparison.

Broadly speaking, it was the goal of self-culture to make it possible for the moments to characterize the days, as it were; to develop a sense of spirituality in every day life. The Transcendentalists sought this in a variety of ways. First and foremost, they looked to nature as a source of revelations concerning the spiritual life. As Thoreau noted characteristically in his Journal: "My profession is always to be on the alert to find God in nature, to know his lurking places, to attend all the oratorios, the operas in nature. . . . To watch for, describe, all the divine features which I detect in Nature."

Emerson, too, looked to nature for spiritual insight and moral instruction. As he observed in one of his lectures on "Human Culture":

We divorce ourselves from nature; we hide ourselves in cities and lose the affecting spectacle of the Day and Night which she cheers and instructs her children withal. We pave the earth for miles with stones and forbid the grass. We build street on street all round the horizon and shut out the sky and the wind; false and costly tastes are generated for wise and cheap ones; thousands are poor and cannot see the face of the world; the senses are impaired, and the susceptibility to beauty; and life made vulgar. Our feeling in the presence of nature is an admonishing hint. Go and hear in a woodland valley the harmless roarings of the South wind and see the shining boughs of the trees in the sun, the swift sailing clouds, and you shall think man is a fool to be mean and unhappy when every day is made illustrious by these splendid shows. Then falls the enchanting night: all the trees are wind-harps: out shine the stars, and we say, blessed by light and darkness, ebb and flow, cold and heat, these restless pulsations of nature which throb for us. In the presence of nature a man of feeling is not suVered to lose sight of the instant creation. The world was not made a long while ago. Nature is an Eternal Now.

I quote this passage at length because it is so indicative of the "theology," so to speak, of Natural Religion. Nature is celebrated not solely for its beauty, but also for what it has to teach us about natural order of things and the way we might live our lives. There is a charm and innocence in Emerson's writing that many people find a little naive today. Our fascination with disaster films shows that nature has a darker and more destructive side for us than Emerson himself was inclined to acknowledge. Nevertheless, I think we can agree with Emerson and his Transcendentalist companions that wisdom consists in conforming one's life, so far as possible, with the forces and rhythms of the natural world. We are, after all, a product of nature, and the cause of so many of our problems is that we are alienated from it.

If we can have confidence in our instincts and intuitions, as Emerson insisted, it is because we are part and parcel of nature. In the privacy of his Journal, where such heresies might go undetected, Emerson confided: "God resides not in formal religion, but in nature; not in rites, but persons. I grow in God. I am only a form of him. He is the soul of me. I can even with a mountainous aspiring say, I am God." If Emerson was a theist, he was a *pan-theist*. The divine subsists in all of creation, and the soul of nature is coincident with the human soul.

Pantheism is a highly charged theological term. It is usually employed as an epithet, to the extent that no one wants to be accused of being a pantheist or soft on pantheism. Judging by its etymology, the word means, simply, that God is in everything, that is to say, immanent in the world and not transcendent or separate from it. No doubt there was a variety of opinions among the Transcendentalists as to whether God had an existence apart from the universe, but they were agreed that God was revealed in all the creatures and manifestations of the natural world. It was the belief that there is something of God in all of nature and humanity that gave impetus to their considerable efforts in the areas of abolitionism, women's suffrage and conservation.

Because of their pantheist views, the Transcendentalists were inclined to believe that there is a "correspondence" between nature and human nature, between the macrocosm of the universe and the microcosm of the individual human being, between the Ultimate and the finite. This concept had at least two implications. First of all, it meant that there was no fundamental break between the sacred and the secular; therefore all of human existence was religious. Secondly, it suggested that the goal of the religious life was to achieve a sense of harmony with the workings of the cosmos itself.

In pursuing this goal the Transcendentalists engaged in a number of different spiritual practices and techniques, which I will describe momentarily. But before I do I wish to say once more that my interest here is not merely an academic one. The Transcendentalists earnestly sought to address some of the same issues we are dealing with today. Like us, they were trying to integrate their ideals with everyday living. Like us, they questioned the prevailing values of society. Like us, they struggled to achieve a loftier perspective from which to resolve the problems of life.

The extent to which they were successful in these efforts is largely due to the tenacity by which they pursued self-culture. Their lives were certainly no easier than ours; if anything, they were more difficult. The pressures to find a career and make a living were just as great. It was a struggle even to afford an education, to marry and raise a family. Opportunities—especially for women—were limited. And the mid-nineteenth century experienced the longest work-week of any period for which we have records.

Nevertheless, the Transcendentalists and their followers placed a high priority on the cultivation of the soul. It was—and still is—the key to happiness, at least in the Jeffersonian sense of the term. They discovered that the combination of what Emerson referred to as "plain living and high thinking" offered the conditions most favorable to the active pursuit of leisure—leisure not as free time but self-culture. In some ways, perhaps, it was easier for them. Although they were progressive and forward-looking—suspicious if not dismissive of tradition and received wisdom—they still valued the classics, especially Plato and the Neo-Platonic and Stoic philosophers. From these writers they learned the importance of spiritual growth and self-discovery, and the wisdom of trying to achieve a sense of balance and proportion in life.

I think we can learn from the Transcendentalists, even as they benefited from previous models. Often when I talk about Transcendentalist spirituality, people tell me that they find the message an attractive but impractical one. There is a certain wistfulness in the response, as if to say I wish I could, but I can't. I reply that the care of the soul is not easy. As Thoreau remarked in *Walden*, moral reform—by which he meant spiritual awareness—"is the effort to throw off sleep." Our own condition is more a state of drowsiness than anything else. It's as though we are living in a fog a great deal of the time. If we were able to rouse ourselves from the spiritual stupor we find ourselves so habitually in, perhaps it would be more clear to us the direction in which our life lies.

How to wake up, to achieve spiritual awareness, and as a result enable the moments of insight to characterize the days of our lives—this is an issue as much for us as for the Transcendentalists. The Transcendentalists pursued self-culture in a whole host of ways, including contemplation, journal-writing, "conversations," reading and sauntering in the out-of-doors. Let's take a closer look at these spiritual practices of the Transcendentalists. Maybe they will have some appeal and use for us as well. I think we will find that they are especially congenial to a Unitarian Universalist religious sensibility. They are, after all, a product of our own history and spiritual temperament.

⑥

Over the years, I have changed my mind concerning the nature and object of religion. It may sound heretical to say so, but I have come to believe that religion is not so much about thinking as it is about living. It is not so much about meaning as it is about passion. It is not so much about doctrines as it is about waking up, about being fully alive, in the awareness of the present moment. I agree with what Ralph Waldo Emerson wrote in his Journal. Religion, he said, is neither beliefs nor rituals. It is life. "It is not something else to be *got*, to be *added*, but is a new life of those faculties which you have."

I have been led to this conclusion largely by my reading of the Transcendentalists. The insistence that every moment is precious, that we must make the most of each one of them, that the greatest challenge of life is to wake up before we die, and that this is what religion is really all about—these are characteristic of Transcendentalist spirituality, and part of the lasting legacy of Transcendentalism.

This is the message of Emerson's poem "Days." The days of our lives offer us gifts which we may accept or refuse. Forgetting his "morning wishes"—that is to say, his youthful dreams—Emerson takes only a few herbs and apples. Too late does he realize the lost opportunity. The same is true for us, I venture to say.

For his part Thoreau said, "In any weather, at any hour of the day or night, I have been anxious to improve the nick of time, and notch it on my stick, too; to stand at the meeting of two eternities, the past and the future, which is precisely the present moment, and to toe that line." He knew—as we should also know—that only in the present moment can there be happiness or change or growth. Life itself exists only in the here and now. "We are always getting ready to live," Emerson said. There "is very little life in a lifetime." Only by making the most of each moment can we be assured of living life to its fullest. This may seem obvious or even superficial. When we're young and it appears we have our whole life in front us, we think we have plenty of time to spare. As we get older, however, there is a poignant urgency to savor experience as completely as possible.

As with so many things, unfortunately, this is easier said than done. Awareness is obviously the key. The best way—indeed the only way—to capture moments is to pay attention. Attentiveness means waking up. Although this may seem simple, it is not necessarily easy. Our habitual lack of awareness, our tendency to be distracted and dissatisfied, keeps us pretty well anesthetized. To wake up, to achieve awareness, takes discipline. It takes practice. This is what the care of the soul is all about.

Many religious traditions prescribe meditation or prayer or physical deprivations of some sort. No doubt these can be very effective, but not if they are a form of straining or running after special insights or visions. We cannot force ourselves to be relaxed. Becoming aware means simply being present in the moment. We are not trying to improve ourselves or to get anywhere else. We can do this in any place at any time, taking each moment as it comes. This is what I call contemplation—a practice, as it were, more congenial to my own spiritual temperament.

Thoreau went to Walden Pond as a personal experiment in developing attentiveness. Walden Pond is a beautiful place, made all the more special by virtue of its association with Concord's favorite son. But we don't really need to go out of our way or even find some place special to practice awareness. Walden Pond can be anywhere. While he was there, Thoreau would often sit in his doorway for hours and simply watch and listen as the sun moved across the sky and the light and shadows changed almost imperceptibly. He describes it this way:

> There were times when I could not afford to sacrifice the bloom of the present moment to any work, whether of the head or hand. I love a broad margin to my life. Sometimes, on a summer morning, having taken my accustomed bath, I sat in my sunny doorway from sunrise till noon . . . amidst the pines and hickories and sumacs, in undisturbed solitude and stillness, while the birds sang around or flitted noiseless through the house, until by the sun falling in my west window, or the noise of some traveler's wagon on the distant highway, I was reminded of the lapse of time. I grew in those seasons like corn in the night, and they were far better than any work of the hands would have been. They were not time subtracted from my life, but so much over and above my usual allowance. I realized what the Orientals mean by contemplation and the forsaking of works.

For me, as for the Transcendentalists, the religious life has a lot to do with cultivating a sense of the miraculous and with recognizing the interconnectedness of all things. Both of these are essentially a matter of perception, and not of belief. Emerson insisted that "the inevitable mark of wisdom is to see the miraculous in the common." When we view the world in this way we see that everything is of a piece, that all things are interconnected. Everything is related to everything else. What is more, everything is in flux. Stars are born, go through stages, and die. So do we. This awareness might truly enhance our appreciation of the world and help us to take things and circumstances and relationships less for granted. We might appreciate life more, people more, moments more, if we perceive, by looking more deeply into them, that everything we are in contact with connects us to the whole world in each fleeting moment.

To savor every moment as it passes is the highest of the arts. Even for those who live it fully, there is only so much life in a lifetime. We must make the most of what we have. If there is eternal life it is not immortality or heaven, but awareness of eternity in this time and this place. "We must live in the present," Thoreau insisted, "launch ourselves on every wave, find our eternity in each moment." Of course, awake or asleep we shall one day die. The difference between a life well lived and one ill-spent has everything to do with taking advantage of the multitude of possibilities that exist in each moment. But if we are asleep—distracted, stressed-out, devoid of feeling—we cannot realize any of these possibilities. We are dying to wake up, to be fully alert and alive in the present, knowing, as Thoreau said, "Only that day dawns to which we are awake."

In keeping with Thoreau's insistence that "we must learn to reawaken and keep ourselves awake," the Transcendentalists engaged in a number of practices aimed at accomplishing this result. These were part and parcel of what they termed the doctrine of self-culture. As you might imagine, they enjoyed the out-of-doors and made a concerted effort to spend a part of every day in an encounter with the natural world. This was for them a spiritual discipline and an experience akin to worship. Emerson was noted for his daily walks. Thoreau went even farther than that: "I think that I cannot preserve my health and spirits unless I spend four hours a day at least . . . sauntering through the woods and over the hills, absolutely free from all worldly engagements."

Sauntering was the term he gave to walking as a spiritual discipline. "The walking of which I speak," he said, "has nothing in it akin to the taking of exercise . . . but is itself the enterprise and adventure of the day. . . . If you would get exercise, go in search of the springs of life." Thoreau rhapsodizes on the subject in his essay, "Walking." The term is derived from vagabonds who roamed the Medieval countryside begging for money on the pretext of going to the Holy Land, or Sainte Terre. Hence, Saunterer or Holy-Lander. "They who never go to the Holy Land in their walks . . . are indeed mere idlers and vagabonds," he said. "For every walk is a sort of crusade, preached by some Peter the Hermit in us, to go forth and reconquor this Holy Land from the hands of the Infidels."

Walking, then, is not mere exercise, nor is it some kind of tour of the neighborhood where we come round at the end of the day to the comforts of home. Indeed, Thoreau set some high standards for being a saunterer, and not everyone qualified. His most trusted companions were fellow Transcendentalists, including Emerson, Alcott and Ellery Channing. For him sauntering was a noble enterprise. "No wealth, " he said, "can buy the requisite leisure, freedom, and independence which are the capital in this profession. It comes only by the grace of God. It requires a direct dispensation from Heaven to become a walker."

In addition to sauntering, which seemed to be a form of walking meditation, Thoreau also undertook what he referred to as *excursions*. These seem to be more purposeful outings which occasioned many of his books and essays—accounts of trips to Canada, Cape Cod, the Maine Woods, and up the Concord and Merrimack Rivers. These writings are a treasury of spiritual insights inspired by his encounters with the natural world. Some of his excursions were undertaken nearer to home and are described in his Journal.

Periods of motion and activity—that is, excursions—alternated with interludes of rest and reverie, or *contemplation*. The two years he spent at Walden Pond were an especially contemplative time for Thoreau. I quoted earlier a passage where he describes a summer morning where he sat "rapt in a revery" from sunrise till noon. Contemplation was a spiritual exercise for Emerson as well. A silent stream of thoughts descend to us from above, he observed in his lectures on "Human Culture," and he advised spiritual seekers to keep a "religious eye turned to this upward light," attending to it with what he called, "lowly expectation":

> The simple habit of sitting alone occasionally to explore what facts of moment lie in the memory may have the effect in some more favored hour to open to the student the kingdom of spiritual nature. He may become aware that there around him roll new at this moment and inexhaustible the waters of Life; that the world he has lived in so heedless, so gross, is illuminated with meaning, that every fact is magical; every atom alive, and he is the heir of it all.

Reading was another form of spiritual discipline for the Transcendentalists. All of them were voracious readers. Thoreau had a chapter devoted to the subject in *Walden*. As with everything else he did, Thoreau approached reading with a certain athleticism, which we see in this passage:

> To read well, that is to read true books in a true spirit, is a noble exercise, and one that will task the reader more than any exercise which the customs of the day esteem. It requires a training such as the athletes underwent, the steady intention almost of the whole life to this object. Books must be read as deliberately and reservedly as they were written.

Emerson and Parker were known for their extensive libraries. Margaret Fuller was a discerning reader and literary critic. Alcott and Thoreau compiled lengthy lists of the books they had read. Mostly, they read for spiritual insights, or "lustres," as Emerson called them.

Their reading included poetry, philosophy, mythology, history, science and biography. They were especially attracted to the classics, and to the sacred texts of other religious traditions, including those of the Near East, India and China. In the Dial, a Transcendentalist publication edited by Fuller and Emerson, was a column devoted to "Ethnical Scriptures" from the world's religions. They were inspired by these, and found that they confirmed the truth of their own spiritual views. Because they felt the Universal Spirit present in all times and places, they looked for—and discovered—evidence of it in all religious faiths. This impulse led to some of the earliest efforts in comparative religious studies, including multi-volume works by Lydia Maria Child, James Freeman Clarke and Samuel Johnson, all of them Transcendentalists.

The Transcendentalists also engaged in the spiritual exercise of *writing*. Virtually all of them wrote, lectured or preached, and most of them kept a journal or diary. Emerson, Thoreau and Alcott are especially noted for having kept journals. Certainly the best of Alcott is in his journals and many feel the same about Thoreau. Emerson began writing his journal at the age of seventeen, when he was still a student at Harvard. And it was with Emerson's encouragement that Thoreau began his own journal in 1837. In the lectures on "Human Culture," Emerson also commented on the virtues of journal-keeping:

Pay so much honor to the visits of Truth in your mind as to record those thoughts that have shown therein. . . . It is not for what is recorded, though that may be the agreeable entertainment of later years, and the pleasant remembrances of what we were, but for the habit of rendering account to yourself of yourself in some more rigorous manner and at certain intervals than mere conversation or casual reverie of solitude require.

Aside from keeping a journal as a means of promoting his own self-culture—a journal, incidentally, that he kept for over fifty years, and running to more than five million words—Bronson Alcott made the concept of self-culture the cornerstone of his theories and methods of education. His treatise on *The Doctrine and Discipline of Human Culture* was written as a rationale for his work with children at the Temple School in Boston. Later on he applied the concept to the education of adults by means of what he termed *conversations*. Alcott rejected traditional instructional methods in favor of conversations as a pedagogical tool. These conversations were akin to Socratic dialogues. "Conversation," he wrote in his Journal, is "the natural organ of communicating, mind with mind. . . . It is the method of human culture. By it I come nearer to the hearts of those to whom I . . . address than by any other means."

Emerson, Thoreau, Fuller, Alcott and Elizabeth Peabody (who introduced kindergartens to America) had all been teachers at one time or another. For them, as for the Transcendentalists generally, education was a process in which persons were engaged in recollecting what, in some sense, they already knew; or, as Alcott put it, "drawing truth from the facts of common experience rather than from the history of opinions as set forth in the systems of philosophy or creeds of theologians." As you might well imagine, with thoughts like these none of them were employed as teachers for long. Their ideas were simply too heretical for the times.

Nevertheless, leading groups of adults in conversation on various subjects was a source of livelihood for Alcott, and he held courses of conversations in many neighboring towns. In later years, when he had become something of an icon in educational circles, Alcott led conversations during his travels to the American Midwest. Margaret

Fuller also led conversations, primarily with groups of women, as a means of producing income and promoting self-culture. For a period of five years she conducted conversations on such topics as mythology, education, women's issues and universal religious ideas.

These spiritual disciplines—sauntering and excursions, contemplation, reading, journal writing and conversations—were all methods for the cultivation of the soul. But in keeping with the doctrine of self-culture, these means were never ends in themselves. The Transcendentalists held that spirituality required an outward manifestation of inward aspirations. In other words, the moral and the spiritual were necessarily interrelated. Accordingly, the Transcendentalists sought to achieve a congruence between spiritual insights and ethical actions in all areas of their lives. This was most notable in their experiments in *simple living* and their involvements with social and religious *reforms*.

It was the Transcendentalists' common goal to develop ways of living that reduced their material needs to a minimum so that they would be freer to pursue leisure—that is to say, spiritual truths, moral ideals and aesthetic impulses. The experimental quality of these efforts can be seen in Thoreau's cabin at Walden Pond and George Ripley's commune at Brook Farm.

Thoreau built his famous cabin at Walden Pond in 1845 and lived there for a little over two years. In *Walden* he gave an account of his daily life and his reasons for going there. Basically, he wanted to simplify his life and find time for writing—as he put it, "to transact some private business with the fewest obstacles." He lamented the fact that his fellow citizens were so preoccupied with material concerns that they had no time for leisure. Thoreau was determined to redress this imbalance in his own life by practicing a voluntary poverty and cultivating spiritual awareness. He concluded from his efforts that:

> . . . if one advances confidently in the direction of his dreams, and endeavors to live the life which he has imagined, he will meet with a success unexpected in common hours. He will put some things behind, will pass an invisible boundary; new, universal, and more liberal laws will begin to establish themselves around and within him;

or the old laws will be expanded and interpreted in his favor in a more liberal sense, and he will live with the license of a higher order of beings.

For his part, George Ripley quit the Unitarian ministry in 1840 to found the Brook Farm Institute for Education and Agriculture. This was a cooperative community consisting of teachers, students and workers engaged in the labor of farming and the pursuit of self-culture. Members of the community sought a balance in their lives between work and leisure. In a letter to Emerson, Ripley indicated that the reason for his undertaking was "to prepare a society of liberal, intelligent and cultivated persons, whose relations with each other would permit a more simple and wholesome life, than can be led amidst the pressure of our competitive institutions."

Although Emerson did not elect to join the others at Brook Farm, he did visit from time to time, as did Alcott, Fuller, Elizabeth Peabody and many of their Transcendentalist comrades. The commune lasted for six years and included, in the early years, about 150 adults and children. Poets, philosophers, ministers, reformers, artists and writers worked together doing farm work. Wages were the same for all and free time was spent in contemplation and creative pursuits. One of the Brook Farmers later recalled that most of the residents "were happy, contented, well-off, carefree; doing a great work in the world, enthusiastic and faithful. We enjoyed every moment of every day."

In a more modest experiment, Emerson had moved to the village of Concord so that he could afford to live on his income as a writer and lecturer. And in a more extreme one, Alcott risked family and fortune on an ill-fated attempt to found the Fruitlands commune. But, modest or extreme, solitary or communal, successful or ill-fated, these undertakings represented some of the Transcendentalists' practical experiments in self-culture. They were indicative of the goal of the spiritual life as they came to envision it; namely, in Emerson's phrase, "plain living and high thinking."

By high thinking they did not mean intellectualism as such. The Transcendentalists were, on the whole, well-educated and intelligent people. They were writers and thinkers and artists and reformers. They valued the intellect. But high thinking had more to do with contemplation, with higher thoughts, than with erudition. It was more in keeping with what Thoreau referred to as "philosopher's simplicity"—"outwardly simple; inwardly complex." A number of the Transcendentalists drafted credos, or simple statements of their life's purpose. William Henry Channing, nephew of the great William Ellery, titled his "My Symphony":

> To live content with small means; to seek elegance rather than luxury, and refinement rather than fashion; to be worthy, not respectable, and wealthy, not rich; to study hard, think quietly, talk gently, act frankly; to listen to stars and birds, to babes and sages with an open heart; to bear all cheerfully, do all bravely, await occasions, never hurry. In a word, to let the spiritual, unbidden and unconscious, grow up through the common. This is to be my symphony.

What is to be our credo, our philosophy of life in a nutshell? Each of us must write our own symphony and work out our own destiny in our own way. But I would suggest that we might begin by taking to heart this advice from *Walden,* still a classic on living the spiritual life:

> When he has obtained those things which are necessary to life, there is another alternative than to obtain the superfluities; and that is to adventure on life now, his vacation from humbler toil having commenced. The soil, it appears, is suited to the seed, for it has sent its radicle downward, and it may now send its shoot upward also with confidence. Why has man rooted himself thus firmly in the earth, but that he may rise in the same proportion into the heavens above?

The problems of contemporary living are serious ones, made more difficult by the fact that we are so accustomed to them, and therefore more inclined towards accommodation than change. Old habits and customary ways of doing things are always roadblocks to self-culture. But, as Thoreau said, "it is never too late to give up our prejudices"; and though the life of the spirit is threatened by the materialism of our day, it is by no means dead. There is too much evidence to the contrary. Indeed, we are witnessing a flowering of the spirit, even in Unitarian Universalist circles.

I wish there was more time for us to explore these matters. I can only suggest at this point that in the lives and writings of the Transcendentalists we will find a model for cultivating the soul in keeping with our Unitarian Universalist faith. Large numbers of men and women, themselves inspired to some extent by Emerson and Thoreau, have found a spiritual home in our congregations, dimly aware, most of them, of the historical connection. There is in our Transcendentalist heritage the source of a uniquely and authentically Unitarian Universalist spirituality. In claiming this inheritance for ourselves we will discover both the possibility of a deeper, richer inner life and a stronger sense of religious identity as Unitarian Universalists.

❁

Walden, by Henry David Thoreau, is a spiritual classic. One of the best-selling books of all time, it has appeared in over 200 editions since it was first published in 1854. It has been translated into every major language. But what kind of book is it? Like all great literature, it can be read in different ways. Noted Thoreau scholar Walter Harding indicates five of them.

It can be read as a nature book. Its original subtitle was "life in the woods," and is filled with observations on nature through the seasons of the year. Even today, the book is often found in the Nature section of local bookstores. Indeed, *Walden* is considered a classic in the field of natural history and the standard by which subsequent nature writing has been judged.

Many of the book's fans have read it as a do-it-yourself guide to living the simple life. Thoreau has seemed to be the champion of a counter-cultural alternative to the materialism of American society from his time to ours. He does not advocate "dropping out," but finding a healthy balance between solitude and society, nature and civilization, materialism and a life of voluntary poverty.

The book has also been appreciated for its satirical criticism of modern life. *Walden* is a biting, tongue-in-cheek critique of American society, full of irony, wit and hyperbole. Thoreau has a great sense of humor and enjoys poking fun of his neighbors and fellow townspeople. His is not humor for its own sake, but is aimed at the reform of existing institutions and customs.

Walden is a well-crafted work of good literature. Thoreau is often credited with writing the first modern American prose. There is much to admire about his writing style: his composition, his allusiveness, his use of fable, symbolism and parody, his employment of the language. He is part of the American literary canon largely because professors in departments of literature consider him a great writer.

Yet another way of reading the book is as a religious classic, a guidebook to the spiritual life. This, I believe, is how Thoreau himself meant it to be read. He and his fellow Transcendentalists felt they were writing modern-day scripture to promote what they termed "self-culture," the cultivation of the soul. First and foremost, *Walden* is a book about spiritual renewal and reformation, and this is how we will approach it in this guide.

Like other religious texts, *Walden* invites study and frequent reading. I try to re-read the book at least once a year. I find new depths of meaning each time I do so—lines and passages I had overlooked before, but which now speak to me. And like a pilgrim with a holy book, I find that I often bring a copy of *Walden* with me on my "excursions," as Thoreau would call them. Now as then, Thoreau is a wonderful travelling companion.

Suggested Reading

Harding, Walter, *The Days of Henry David Thoreau*, Knopf, 1965.

Paul, Sherman, *The Shores of America: Thoreau's Inward Exploration*, University of Illinois Press, 1958.

Richardson, Robert, *Henry David Thoreau: A Life of the Mind*, University of California Press, 1986.

Thoreau, Henry David, *Walden: An Annotated Edition*, Houghton Mifflin, 1995.

⑥

"Conversation as the natural organ of communicating, mind with mind, . . . is the method of human culture. By it I come nearer the hearts of those whom I shall address than by any other means."
— *The Journals of Bronson Alcott*

Beginning in 1839, and continuing for five years thereafter, Margaret Fuller (1810-1850) led a much celebrated and well-attended series of Conversations in the Boston area. These were essentially group discussions, facilitated by Fuller, on a variety of topics, including literature, mythology and women's issues. The series were offered by subscription and consisted of two-hour sessions over a period of three months. Where possible, they were scheduled to coincide with the dates of Ralph Waldo Emerson's lectures in Boston, since both attracted largely the same audience, namely, cultured, well-educated Unitarian women with Transcendentalist leanings. (The attendance at Emerson's lectures included men as well as women; Fuller's Conversations were intended for a female audience.)

The Conversations were held in Elizabeth Peabody's bookstore in downtown Boston. Each series included between twenty-five and thirty-five participants. They proved to be so popular that Fuller added more of them to her increasingly busy schedule. These were not simply intellectual discussions, however, and their purpose was not educational in the traditional sense of the term. Fuller sought, first of all, to integrate the head and the heart, the intellect and the affections. Secondly, she wished to connect learning with living by applying thought to the problems of life. In short, the aim of these Conversations was to promote self-culture as she understood it. She was guided in her efforts by two fundamental questions: "What were we meant to do? How shall we do it?"

In keeping with this aim, the Conversations encouraged intro-spection, originality, and self-reliance. They employed the Socratic method, applied to groups—a multi-logue or poly-logue, as op-posed to a dialogue—facilitated by a leader, in this case Margaret Fuller. And while the leader might begin the session by posing a question for the group to reflect upon and respond to, her role was essentially to facilitate the group discussion that followed. From time to time, of course, the facilitator would need to guide the conversa-tion back to the topic of the day.

It is the "conversation" model that is recommended for this class. In fact, it could easily be described as a Conversation on *Walden*, the purpose of which is not a critical analysis of the book, but a wrestling with the questions it raises for us personally in relation to the way we live our lives today. There is much to admire in Thoreau's writing style, and much to understand about what he means in certain ob-scure passages, but the intention of the class is to engage the partici-pants at a deep level with the issues that Thoreau raises concerning self-culture and the purpose of life. It is the facilitator's role to bring the conversation back, as often as necessary, to a personal encounter with these issues. It was Thoreau's intention to be provocative, "to brag as lustily as chanticleer in the morning . . . if only to wake my neighbors up." The leader must encourage the group to reflect deeply and respond thoughtfully.

In more practical terms, the facilitator of this course will need to be familiar with the assigned readings, having read them carefully ahead of class. The chapter summaries are provided as an aid in identifying Thoreau's major themes and following his line of thought. Each session should begin by summarizing the assigned reading, allowing for comments and clarification, and then proceed by posing as many of the questions for discussion as time permits. The facilitator is expected to stimulate reflection and dialogue, and to keep the conversation from digressing, not to lecture or attempt to answer every question that is asked.

The class leader will need to take care of necessary arrangements for the class, including room set-up, seating (chairs in a circle), chalice-lighting materials, and so on. This will require arriving early to the sessions. It is important to inform participants of the need to arrive on time, to read the assigned material for each class, to speak only for themselves, to allow everyone an equal opportunity to speak, and to refrain from interrupting while others are talking. Because the "conversation" is essentially a facilitated group discussion, it is recommended that attendance be limited to twelve to fifteen people. By no means should the class be larger than twenty.

If there are individuals who are dominating the discussion by talking frequently or at great length the facilitator will need take a firmer hand in guiding the discussion. Make sure that every person has an opportunity to respond to a particular question or topic before someone who has already spoken once is allowed to speak again. Invite those who have not yet spoken to do so, but also respect their right to "pass." Encourage people to raise their hand to speak. Once in a while you may need to interrupt someone who is talking excessively to remind them that others also need to have a chance to speak.

⑥

"I am convinced, both by faith and experience, that to maintain one's self on this earth is not a hardship but a pastime, if we will live simply and wisely."

READING "ECONOMY"

⑥

I think we may safely trust a good deal more than we do. We may waive just so much care of ourselves as we honestly bestow elsewhere. Nature is as well adapted to our weakness as to our strength. The incessant anxiety and strain of some is a well-nigh incurable form of disease. We are made to exaggerate the importance of the work we do; and yet how much is not done by us! Or what if we had been taken sick? How vigilant we are! Determined not to live by faith if we can avoid it; all the day long on the alert, at night we unwillingly say our prayers and commit ourselves to uncertainties. So thoroughly and sincerely are we compelled to live, reverencing our life and denying the possibility of change. This is the only way, we say; but there are as many ways as there can be drawn radii from one centre. All change is a miracle to contemplate; but it is a miracle which is taking place every second. —HDT

At first glance, it seems a little odd that Thoreau would begin his book on life in the woods with a chapter entitled, "Economy." In fact, the chapter is more in the nature of a preface in which he addresses the reasons for writing the book in the first place. As he says in the first few paragraphs, villagers had been asking questions about his stay at Walden Pond, which he proposes to answer. But his primary reason for writing the book is to examine the way most people seem to be spending their lives. As a writer, Thoreau enjoys word play— in this case, the play on words of "Economy," an "accounting" of his two years at Walden Pond, and an examination of the way we "spend" our lives.

"Economy" is the longest chapter in the book, amounting to more than a quarter of its length. It is divided into several subdivisions, the first of which consists of observations on what Thoreau considers to be the common mode of life. "I have travelled a good deal in Concord," he writes, "and everywhere, in shops, and offices, and fields, the inhabitants have appeared to me to be doing penance in a thousand remarkable ways."

People seem so burdened with cares and labors that they cannot enjoy the finer fruits of life. Lacking leisure, they have no time to be anything but a machine. Worst of all, they are driving themselves, as though they had no other choice. Unfortunately, what we think of ourselves determines our fate. Resigned to their apparent lot in life, the mass of people lead lives of quiet desperation.

One might assume that people had deliberately chosen to live this way. In fact, they think there is no alternative. But, Thoreau insists, "it is never too late to give up our prejudices." Change *is* possible. It's just that we're too timid and unsure of what might happen if we followed his advice. Thoreau says that our capacities for change haven't been measured because they've largely been untried. He insists that we may safely trust a good more than we do. Our incessant anxiety is an incurable form of disease. "How vigilant we are!" he says, "determined not to live by faith if we can avoid it." We feel so compelled to live the way we do that we deny the possibility of change: "This is the only way, we say; but there are as many ways as there can be drawn radii from one centre. All change is a miracle to contemplate; but it is a miracle which is taking place every second."

Thoreau's immediate reason for going to live at Walden Pond was to find the time and solitude he needed to write a book about a trip he and his brother, John, had taken up the Concord and Merrimack Rivers a couple of years before. But, in a larger sense, he conceived of his stay there as an experiment in simple living, with the intention of discovering the "necessaries of life" and what it takes to obtain them. He defines "necessaries" as those things which, once secured, will enable us to "entertain the true problems of life with freedom and a prospect of success." Never satisfied, however, with securing the necessities only, we reach for the luxuries, which Thoreau considers positive hindrances to our spiritual elevation. The wisest, he says, have always lived in voluntary poverty.

Indeed, when we have obtained the necessities of life, there is an alternative to going after the superfluities, Thoreau argues, and that is "to adventure on life now, [our] vacation from humbler toil having commenced." Once we have our physical needs met, it is time to seek a deeper, more spiritual kind of fulfillment. Thoreau does not quarrel with those who feel well-employed. He is mainly concerned with those who feel otherwise, complaining of their lot in life when they might actually improve it, those who feel trapped out of a sense of duty, and those who have accumulated possessions and are now feeling burdened by them.

In the next brief section of the chapter Thoreau tells how he has spent his own life. As much as possible he has tried to live extemporaneously, in the present moment: "In any weather, at any hour of the day or night, I have been anxious to improve the nick of time, and notch it on my stick, too; to stand at the meeting of two eternities, the past and the future, which is precisely the present moment; to toe that line." In a cryptic but intriguing passage, he says "I long ago lost a hound, a bay horse, and a turtle-dove, and am still on their trail." These are symbolic of his losses in life, which he is still trying to recover. He has spent much of his time in the out-of-doors, greeting the sunrise, and acting as a "self-appointed inspector of snow-storms and rain-storms." He concludes by saying that his purpose in going to Walden Pond "was not to live cheaply nor to live dearly there, but to transact some private business with the fewest obstacles."

The following section deals at considerable length with two of the "necessaries of life" which Thoreau has identified, clothing and shelter. His observations on each of these are similar, and anticipate Veblen's remarks on conspicuous consumption. People are so prone to following fads and fashions and to keeping up with their neighbors that they can't be satisfied with what they already have. They must have the latest fashions and ever larger houses. His comments on clothing are especially pointed and humorous. In a well-known passage he warns us "to beware of enterprises that require new clothes, and not rather a new wearer of clothes." He says something similar about shelter; namely, that we have improved our houses but not those who inhabit them. Moreover, the expense involved in purchasing new clothes and big houses entails a considerable sacrifice since, in Thoreau's view, "the cost of a thing is the amount of what I will call life which is required to be exchanged for it immediately or in the long run." Thus, in the case of clothing and shelter, we "spend" time that we could be putting to better and higher uses on what are essentially superficial and superfluous pursuits.

For Thoreau the rise of the consumption ethic corresponds with a fall from an original state of grace and innocence. In more primitive times, when humans dwelt in tents as it were, it was more obvious that we were "sojourners in Nature." Now, he says, we "have settled down on earth and forgotten heaven." We have become captive of our possessions; our mansions have become our tombs. The best works of art used to elevate us from this condition. Now the arts have been corrupted to make our "low estate comfortable and that higher state to be forgotten."

In a more strict accounting of dollars and cents, Thoreau provides a detailed description of the building of his cabin at Walden Pond. He wants his readers to know that it is possible to provide for one's shelter without mortgaging one's freedom. He makes a similar accounting of how he managed to support himself and meet his needs while he was there. In passing, he makes comments about "modern improvements," which he considers "improved means to unimproved ends," which distract our attention from more serious matters. (He mentions the telegraph and the railroad in this context, but would have undoubtedly said the same about the automobile and e-mail.) The point being that we spend the best part of our lives earning money in order "to enjoy a questionable liberty" in our retirement.

Thoreau concludes his assessment by reckoning that for the past five years he has supported himself on the earnings of six weeks' labor per year. The rest of the time he had "free and clear" to pursue the project of his own self-culture. As a result of his efforts to minimize his needs in order to maximize his leisure, he was convinced "both by faith and experience, that to maintain one's self on this earth is not a hardship but a pastime, if we will live simply and wisely." However, he cautioned others against imitating his mode of life—or their parents or neighbors—insisting that each person find and follow his or her own way.

In a coda to the chapter, Thoreau makes a few pointed comments about philanthropy. Evidently some of his neighbors accused him of being selfish in his pursuit of leisure. If he had nothing else to do, they said, he might as well have done some charitable work. He replies that he has done charity, but has no "genius" for it. Moreover, he is suspicious of philanthropists and reformers who are merely "do-gooders." "If you give money," he says, "spend yourself with it and do not merely abandon it to them." As for reform, in most cases it does not go far enough: "There are a thousand hacking at the branches of evil, to one who is striking at the root." Thoreau believes that benevolence should be "the flower and fruit" of a person, that our "goodness must not be a partial and transitory act, but a constant superfluity," which costs us little and of which we are largely unconscious.

⑥

Whenever I return from a sojourn in the woods or waters or mountains, I'm dismayed by the noise and jumble of the workaday world. One moment I can lay everything I need on the corner of a poncho, tally my responsibilities on the fingers of one hand. The next moment, it seems, I couldn't fit all my furniture and tasks into a warehouse. Time in the wild reminds me how much of what I ordinarily do is mere dithering, how much of what I own is mere encumbrance. Coming home, I can see that there are too many appliances in my cupboards, too many clothes in my closet, too many strings of duty jerking me in too many directions. The opposite of simplicity, as I understand it, is not complexity but clutter.

Returning from a backcountry trip, I vow to purchase nothing that I don't really need, give away everything that is excess, refuse all chores that don't arise from central concerns. The simplicity I seek is not the enforced austerity of the poor. I seek instead the richness of a gathered life, which comes from letting one's belongings and commitments be few in number and high in quality.

—Scott Russell Sanders, "The Stuff of Life"

Questions for Discussion

- In the opening paragraphs of the chapter, Thoreau observes that people seem so burdened with cares and labors that they cannot enjoy "the finer fruits of life." They have no leisure nor time to be anything but a machine. To what extent do you think Thoreau's observation is true of life today? How much leisure do you have? In Thoreau's view leisure was for the pursuit of self-culture, the cultivation of the soul. How do you "spend" your leisure time? What, for you, are "the finer fruits of life"?

- Thoreau says that people are too accepting of their perceived lot in life and underestimate their capacity for change. Do you agree? Have you made any conscious changes in the way you live your life? Thoreau says we are "determined not to live by faith if we can avoid it." What would it mean to you "to live by faith"?

- Thoreau insists that when we have obtained the necessities of life, there is an alternative to going after the superfluities, and that is "to adventure on life now, [our] vacation from humbler toil having commenced." What are the necessities of life for you? How do you know when you've obtained them? How do you know when enough is enough? If you were "to adventure on life now," what would this mean for you?

- What do you think Thoreau means in the passage that begins, "I long ago lost a hound, a bay horse, and a turtle dove, and am still on their trail?" What are some things you have lost and are still looking for?

- Thoreau is critical of so-called modern improvements that merely seem to be "improved means to unimproved ends." What do you think he means by this? Can you think of any contemporary examples?

- "I am convinced, both by faith and experience, that to maintain one's self on this earth is not a hardship but a pastime, if we will live simply and wisely." Do you agree? What does it mean to you to "live simply and wisely?"

- Evidently some of Thoreau's neighbors felt that his experiment in simple living was selfish and that if he had so much time on his hands, he should be doing some charitable work instead. Do you believe that the pursuit of self-culture and a concern for the welfare of others are antithetical? How do you balance the two in your own life?

- "If our addiction to growth is rooted in evolutionary history, we can't just decide to feel good about living with less. We can, however, shift the focus of our expansionary desires. We can change the standard by which we measure prosperity. We can choose to lead a materially simpler life not as a sacrifice but as a path toward fulfillment. In ancient terms, we can learn to seek spiritual rather than material growth." [Scott Russell Sanders, "The Stuff of Life"] Do you agree with Sanders' comment? Have you made an effort "to seek spiritual rather than material growth?" In what ways, and with what success?

Additional Resources

Andrews, Cecile, *The Circle of Simplicity: Return to the Good Life*, HarperCollins, 1997.

Domingues, Joe and Vicki Robin, *Your Money or Your Life: Transforming Your Relationship with Money and Achieving Financial Independence*, Penguin Books, 1992.

Elgin, Duane, *Voluntary Simplicity: Toward a Way of Life That Is Outwardly Simple, Inwardly Rich*, Quill, 1993.

Rechtschaffen, Stephan, *Timeshifting: Creating More Time to Enjoy Your Life*, Doubleday, 1996.

Sanders, Scott Russell, "The Stuff of Life," Utne Reader, November-December 1998.

Schor, Judith, *The Overspent American: Upscaling, Downshifting, and the New Consumer*, Basic Books, 1998.

HOW DO WE WAKE UP?

⑥

"The morning wind forever blows, the poem of creation is uninter-
rupted; but few are the ears that hear it. Olympus is but the outside
of the world everywhere."

READING "WHERE I LIVED AND WHAT I LIVED FOR"

⑥

*We must learn to reawaken and keep ourselves awake, not by mechani-
cal aids, but by an infinite expectation of the dawn, which does not for-
sake us in our soundest sleep. I know of no more encouraging fact than the
unquestionable ability of man to elevate his life by a conscious endeavor.
It is something to be able to paint a particular picture, or to carve a statue,
and so to make a few objects beautiful; but it is far more glorious to carve
and paint the very atmosphere and medium through which we look,
which morally we can do. To affect the quality of the day, that is the highest of arts. Every man is tasked to make his life, even in its details, worthy
of the contemplation of his most elevated and critical hour.* —HDT

Chapter Summary

The style and feeling-tone of this chapter is in marked contrast to that
of the previous one. Where "Economy" is polemical, sometimes truc-

ulent, the second chapter is lyrical, often sublime. It contains some of Thoreau's best writing and most elevated thoughts. Sherman Paul, author of *The Shores of America: Thoreau's Inward Exploration*, says that Thoreau's doctrines were directed to the end of joy. We see ample evidence of this in "Where I Lived and What I Lived For."

There is a mythic quality to Thoreau's writing in this chapter, as if to suggest that he is dealing with timeless truths. As he begins to describe where he lived he observes that every spot might be the site of a house, and that wherever one lives, that place becomes the center of the cosmos. It is where we feel centered and grounded. His description alternates between precise information about the location and surroundings of his cabin at Walden Pond and references to mythical times and places, such as Olympus, the steppes of Tartary, classical and Eastern writers, and constellations of stars. "Both time and place were changed," he writes, "and I dwelt nearer to those parts of the universe and to those eras in history which most attracted me." Fully present in the here and now, he felt contemporaneous with the Golden Age of innocence and bliss, which we also might recover if we could only wake up and become more fully aware.

Waking his neighbors up is precisely what Thoreau aims to do. "I do not propose to write an ode to dejection," he says, "but to brag as lustily as chanticleer in the morning, standing on his roost." The morning is the temporal correlative to the cabin site at Walden Pond. In the same way that his hut is a gateway to Olympus, "morning brings back the heroic ages." Morning is a metaphor for spiritual awakening and self-renewal. It is a time of innocence and simplicity:

> Every morning was a cheerful invitation to make my life of equal simplicity, and, I may say innocence, with Nature herself. I have been as sincere a worshiper of Aurora as the Greeks. I got up early and bathed in the pond; that was a religious exercise and one of the best things which I did. They say that characters were graven on the bathing tub of King Tching-thang to this effect: "Renew thyself completely each day; do it again, and again, and forever again."

For Thoreau the morning is the most memorable time of the day. It is the "awakening hour," when "there is the least somnolence in us." The rest of the time we appear to be sleeping. We must rouse ourselves from our spiritual lethargy, not by artificial means, but by aspirations from within which summon us to a higher mode of life. To those who are able to do so, "the day is a perpetual morning." But few are thus awakened. Most are alert enough only for physical labor, considerably fewer for intellectual exertion, fewer still for "a poetic or divine life." It is only when we are awake that we are alive. Thoreau says he has never yet met anyone who was entirely awake.

And yet we can and must make the effort. The yearning for spiritual awakening, like the "infinite expectation of the dawn," is a powerful stimulus. Difficult as it may be, Thoreau is convinced that we have the ability to elevate our lives if we will make a conscious endeavor. "It is something to be able to paint a particular picture," he says, "or to carve a statue, and so to make a few objects beautiful; but it is far more glorious to carve and paint the very atmosphere and medium through which we look, which morally we can do. To affect the quality of the day, that is the highest of arts. Every man is tasked to make his life, even in its details, worthy of the contemplation of his most elevated and critical hour."

Thoreau went to the woods because he wished to live deliberately, fully aware of "the essential facts of life." He wanted to learn the lessons that life had to teach him, "and not," he says, "when I came to die, discover that I had not lived." His purpose was not to practice resignation, unless that proved to be necessary, but:

> to live deep and suck out all that marrow of life, to live so sturdily and Spartan-like as to put to rout all that was not life, to cut a broad swath and shave close, to drive life into a corner, and reduce it to its lowest terms, and, if it proved to be mean, why then to get the whole and genuine meanness of it, and publish its meanness to the world; or if it were sublime, to know it by experience, and be able to give a true account of it in my next excursion.

Unfortunately, we live like ants, our life frittered away by detail. We should try to simplify our lives. Society, as a whole, lives too fast. "Why should we live with such hurry and waste of life?" he asks. "We are determined to be starved before we are hungry. Men say that a stitch in time saves nine, and so they take a thousand stitches today to save nine tomorrow."

People say they want to hear the news, but what passes for news is merely gossip. Like most of our communications, including correspondence, it is superficial. How much more important, Thoreau says, is that which is timeless and real. "Shams and delusions are esteemed for soundest truths, while reality is fabulous." We should pay attention to realities and not allow ourselves to be distracted by appearances. Because of our slumbering and "consenting to be deceived by shows," our daily life of routine and habit is built on illusory foundations. But "when we are unhurried and wise, we perceive that only great and worthy things have any permanent and absolute existence, that petty fears and petty pleasures are but the shadow of the reality." We are like the prince in the Hindu fable who was raised by a forester, ignorant of his true estate. He imagined himself to belong to a lowly caste until one of the king's ministers discovered him and revealed to him who he truly was, thereby dispelling the misconception of his character. We think that our estate, too, is mean, but only because our vision does not penetrate the surface of things. We confuse reality with appearance.

The concluding paragraphs of this chapter are an eloquent summons to wake up and become aware of the marvelous reality that lies about us wherever we are. We think that truth is remote, existing perhaps in some distant place and far off time, but the fact of the matter is that "all these times and places and occasions are now and here," Thoreau says: "God himself culminates in the present moment, and never will be more divine in the lapse of all the ages. And we are enabled to apprehend at all what is sublime and noble only by the perpetual instilling and drenching of the reality that surrounds us."

Therefore, he urges us to spend the day "as deliberately as Nature," determined not to be distracted. Instead of attending to the many trivial demands on our time, we should rather seek more depth in our lives; rather than the delusions of prejudice and appearance, we should seek only reality:

> Let us settle ourselves, and work and wedge our feet downward through the mud and slush of opinion, and prejudice, and tradition, and delusion, and appearance, that alluvion which covers the globe,

through Paris and London, through New York and Boston and Concord, through Church and State, through poetry and philosophy and religion, till we come to a hard bottom and rocks in place, which we call *reality,* and say, This is, and no mistake. . . . Be it life or death, we crave only reality. If we are really dying, let us hear the rattle in our throats and feel cold in the extremities; if we are alive, let us go about our business.

In a particularly poetic passage, Thoreau juxtaposes time and eternity in the metaphor of a stream, evoking something in the way of a mystical experience: "Time is the stream I go a-fishing in. I drink at it; but while I drink I see the sandy bottom and detect how shallow it is. Its thin current slides away, but eternity remains. I would drink deeper; fish in the sky, whose bottom is pebbly with stars. I cannot count one. I know not the first letter of the alphabet. I have always been regretting that I was not as wise as the day I was born."

☙

I find a . . . lesson in the words of the Zen master, Thich Nhat Hanh: "This spot where you sit is your own spot. It is on this very spot and in this very moment that you can become enlightened. You don't have to sit beneath a special tree in a distant land." There are no privileged locations. If you stay put, your place may become a holy center, not because it gives you special access to the divine, but because in your stillness you can hear what might be heard anywhere. All there is to see can be seen from anywhere in the universe, if you knew how to look; and the influence of the entire universe converges on every spot.

—Scott Russell Sanders,
Staying Put: Making a Home in a Restless World

Questions for Discussion

- Where do you feel most at home? How would you describe the experience of being centered and grounded? Might any spot be a place for a home?

- Thoreau aims to wake his neighbors up. He feels that we spend the greater part of our lives asleep. Can you relate to what he is saying? Do you feel that you have been slumbering?

- Do you feel any inward aspiration to live a higher life? What would this mean for you? And how would you go about it?

- Do you think people's attitude affect "the quality of the day?" Does yours? How so? How might you change your attitude?

- What does it mean to live deliberately? Do you feel that you have ever done so? When, and under what circumstances?

- How might you go about simplifying your life? Have you ever tried to do so? Was it difficult for you?

- Thoreau is convinced that we are to a great extent deluded by appearances. How would you describe these appearances as they might characterize some aspect of your life? What is reality for you, and what is illusory?

- How do we wake ourselves up? What might we do? Would you say that you have ever been fully awake? When, and under what circumstances? How would you describe the experience? What difference, if any, has it made in your life?

Additional Resources

Kabat-Zinn, Jon, *Wherever You Go, There You Are: Mindfulness Meditation in Everyday Life*, Hyperion, 1994.

Sanders, Scott Russell, *Staying Put: Making a Home in a Restless World*, Beacon, 1993.

HOW DO WE GROW?

⑥

"Books are the treasured wealth of the world and the fit inheritance of generations and nations."

READING "READING" AND "SOUNDS"

⑥

There were times when I could not afford to sacrifice the bloom of the present moment to any work, whether of the head or the hands. I love a broad margin to my life. Sometimes, in a summer morning, having taken my accustomed bath, I sat in my sunny doorway from sunrise till noon, rapt in a revery, amidst the pines and hickories and summachs, in undisturbed solitude and stillness, while the birds sang around or flitted noiseless through the house, until by the sun falling in at my west window, or the noise of some traveller's wagon on the distant highway, I was reminded of the lapse of time. I grew in those seasons like corn in the night, and they were far better than any work of the hands would have been. They were not time subtracted from my life, but so much over and above my usual allowance. I realized what the Orientals mean by contemplation and the forsaking of works. —HDT

"Reading" is the first chapter in which Thoreau describes his day to day life at Walden Pond. We may infer from the primacy of this chapter and his comments on the subject that reading was an important activity during his time there.

He opens the chapter by saying that we would all prefer to be "students and observers" if given the opportunity. What he means by this is the contemplation of eternal truths rather than the study of mundane matters, for, "in dealing with truth we are immortal, and need fear no change nor accident." Reading, obviously, was a means by which he sought to study the truth, and he considered his solitary residence more conducive to this pursuit than any university.

Reading, however, is not for idle minds in idle hours; for Thoreau it is a spiritual discipline:

> To read well, that is, to read true books in a true spirit, is a noble exercise, and one that will task the reader more than any exercise which the customs of the day esteem. It requires a training such as the athletes underwent, the steady intention almost of the whole life to this object. Books must be read as deliberately and reservedly as they were written.

His recommended reading consists largely of the classics and religious scriptures, for they represent the treasured wealth and cumulative wisdom of the human race. We will be truly rich when we have filled our libraries with "Vedas and Zendavestas and Bibles, with Homers and Dantes and Shakespeares, and all the centuries to come shall have successively deposited their trophies in the forums of the world. By such a pile we may hope to scale heaven at last."

Unfortunately, most read for paltry reasons and know little of reading in a high sense, "as a noble intellectual exercise." In Thoreau's day, as in ours, pot-boilers and romantic novels seems to be the most popular literature. The best books are not read even by those who consider themselves good readers. Who is more illiterate, Thoreau asks, the one who can read but doesn't (or who reads the equivalent of junk food), or the one who cannot read at all? At least the illiterate's mind is unprofaned.

Still, there is in good literature much that speaks directly to our condition, whatever it may be, and which would be of great benefit to us, "would be more salutary than the morning or spring to our lives, and possibly put a new aspect on the face of things for us. How many a man has dated a new era in his life from the reading of a book! The book exists for us, perchance, which will explain our miracles and reveal new ones." With the wisdom that comes from reading we shall learn liberality and overcome the customary provincialism of thought.

We consider ourselves modern and think we are making great strides, but look how little we do for our own self-culture. We need to be provoked, goaded, into expanding our horizons of learning. Our communities provide common schools for children, but, aside from the local Lyceum and public library, little in the way of adult education. "It is time," Thoreau argues, "that we had uncommon schools, that we did not leave off our education when we begin to be men and women. It is time that villages were universities, and their elder inhabitants the fellows of the universities, with leisure, to pursue liberal studies the rest of their lives."

The village should be the patron of the arts; it lacks only magnanimity and refinement. It spends money on what farmers and businessmen value, but thinks it Utopian to spend money for things which the intelligent know to be of greater worth. "In stead of noblemen, let us have noble villages of men. If it is necessary, omit one bridge over the river, and throw one arch at least over the darker gulf of ignorance which surrounds us."

Chapter Summary of "Sounds"

Books, for all their timeless wisdom, are abstract and metaphorical, and deal with experience at second hand. Nothing "can supercede the necessity of being forever on the alert." No course of study, including history, philosophy or poetry, can compare with the practice of awareness, the discipline of attending to what is to be seen at first hand. "Will you be a reader, a student merely," he asks, "or a seer? Read your fate, see what is before you, and walk on into futurity."

Thoreau confesses that he did not have much time for reading during his first summer at the pond, he had beans to hoe. And even when he was not tending his garden, he seems to have spent a good deal of time in contemplation. "There are times," he says, "when I couldn't afford to sacrifice the bloom of the present moment to any work, whether of the head or the hands." He required "a broad margin" to his life, meaning by this that it needed to include periods of leisure as well as study and work. For it is in these contemplative interludes that he experienced spiritual growth. ("I grew in those seasons like corn in the night.")

The time spent in contemplation could not be reckoned in days of the calendar nor hours of the clock. Though his neighbors might have considered it sheer idleness, by the standards of the birds and flowers it was time well spent. Living his life in such a mindful way, in full awareness of himself and his surroundings, Thoreau was led to the conclusion that

> I had this advantage, at least, in my mode of life over those who were obliged to look abroad for amusement, to society and the theater, that my life itself was become my amusement and never ceased to be novel. It was a drama of many scenes and without an end. If we were always, indeed, getting our living, and regulating our lives according to the last and best mode we had learned, we should never be troubled with ennui. Follow your genius closely enough, and it will not fail to show you a fresh prospect every hour.

In this frame of mind, even his chores and housework became a pleasant pastime.

Thoreau goes on to describe in great detail the flora and fauna surrounding his cabin, scenes from his window and along the footpath through the forest. He notices the many kinds of berries growing nearby and the great variety of birds and animals in the area. His observations are interrupted, however, by the sound of the railroad train as it passes by the far shore of the pond. The noise is intrusive and disconcerting, drowning out the sounds of nature and disturbing his revery.

The whistle of the locomotive is a metaphor for the troublesome aspects of civilization and commerce, signaling the arrival of "restless city merchants" within the "circle of the town," heedless of the rhythms of nature and village life. The railroad has seemingly set the whole world in motion and speeded everything up, including conversation. Like civilization itself, it is regular, uniform and inevitable. There is no stopping it. "We have constructed a fate," Thoreau says, "that never steps aside." He displays a grudging admiration of commerce for its enterprise and bravery, and the way it gathers goods from all parts of the world.

With the passing of the train, and "all the restless world" with it, Thoreau feels more alone than ever. Nevertheless, he is attentive to the many sounds which he hears, including "the rattle of a carriage or team along the distant highway," the church bells of nearby towns, the lowing of cows, the chanting of whip-poor-wills, the screeching of owls, the rumbling of wagons over bridges, the baying of dogs, the trump of bull frogs, and the sound of cock-crowing. Thoreau lives alone, in the midst of this vortex of sounds, "a vibration of the universal lyre." There is no gate in his yard, "and no path to the civilized world."

⑥

Henry David Thoreau's two years at Walden Pond were above all a personal experiment in mindfulness. He chose to put his life on the line in order to revel in the wonder and simplicity of present moments. But you don't have to go out of your way to find someplace special to practice mindfulness. It is sufficient to make a little time in your life for stillness and what we call non-doing, and then tune into your breathing.

All of Walden Pond is within your breath. The miracle of the changing seasons is within the breath; your parents and your children are within the breath; your body and your mind are within the breath. The breath is the current connecting body and mind, connecting us with our parents and our children, connecting our body with the outer world's body. It is the current of life. There are nothing but golden fish in this stream. All we need to see them clearly is the lens of awareness.

—Jon Kabat-Zinn, *Wherever You Go, There You Are*

Questions for Discussion

- Reading was a spiritual discipline for Thoreau. He read for eternal truths. What role does reading play in your life? What do you read, and what do you read for?

- Bible is a word meaning library. Thoreau thought we should compile our own bibles, including literature and religious writings of our own choosing. What books would you include in your bible?

- Thoreau was a proponent of adult education. "It is time," he said, "that villages were universities, and their elder inhabitants the fellows of the universities, with leisure to pursue liberal studies the rest of their lives." Do you agree? What have you done to "pursue liberal studies" in your adult life? How might congregations provide such opportunities?

- Thoreau says he needs "a broad margin" to his life. Do you try to provide a broad margin to your life? What are some of the ways you do so?

- Thoreau seems to have spent a good deal of time in contemplation at Walden Pond. How much time do you spend in contemplation? Is there any particular time or place or method that is conducive to your efforts at contemplation?

- Thoreau is ambivalent about civilization and commerce, as evidenced in his comments about the locomotive. Do you share his ambivalence? What would be a suitable metaphor for you of the technological nature of society at the beginning of a new millennium?

- The sound of the locomotive disturbed the "vibration of the universal lyre." To what degree are such vibrations disturbed today by all the sounds of a post-industrial age? Can you still feel the vibrations of the "universal lyre?" Where and under what circumstances?

Denby, David, *Great Books,* Simon and Schuster, 1996.

Emerson, Ralph Waldo, "Books," in *Society and Solitude,* Houghton Mifflin, 1904.

Hanh, Thich Nhat, *The Miracle of Mindfulness,* Beacon Press, 1987.

Kabat-Zinn, Jon, *Wherever You Go, There You Are: Mindfulness Meditation in Everyday Life,* Hyperion, 1994.

Moore, Thomas, *The Re-Enchantment of Everyday Life,* Harper Collins, 1996.

SOCIETY AND SOLITUDE

⑥

"I had three chairs in my house; one for solitude, two for friendship, three for society."

READING "SOLITUDE" AND "VISITORS"

⑥

Any prospect of awakening or coming to life to a dead man makes indifferent all times and places. The place where that may occur is always the same, and indescribably pleasant to all our senses. For the most part we allow only outlying and transient circumstances to make our occasions. They are, in fact, the cause of our distraction. Nearest to all things is that power which fashions their being. Next to us the grandest laws are continually being executed. Next to us is not the workman whom we have hired, . . . but the workman whose work we are. —HDT

Chapter Summary of "Solitude"

One has the impression, from the opening words of this chapter, that Thoreau has settled into life at Walden Pond and has come to feel at one with his surroundings. "I go and come with a strange liberty in Nature, a part of herself," he writes; "all of the elements are unusually congenial to me." At all events, he has lived there long enough

47

that visitors have begun to seek him out, leaving flowers and other mementos as calling cards.

In spite of the occasional visitor, he enjoys a great deal of solitude in his forest retreat. His nearest neighbor is a mile distant and Thoreau is, by his own reckoning, the sole inhabitant of the Walden woods. "I have, as it were, my own sun and moon and stars, and a little world all to myself." In spite of his isolation, he was at home in nature and seldom "felt lonesome, or in the least oppressed by a sense of solitude." Some of his most pleasant hours were those spent indoors during lengthy rainstorms or on long winter evenings "in which many thoughts had time to take root and unfold themselves."

In solitude he felt most connected to his spiritual roots:

> What do we most want to dwell near to? Not to many men surely, the depot, the post-office, the bar-room, the meeting-house, the school-house, the grocery, Beacon Hill or the Five Points, where men most congregate, but to the perennial source of our life, whence in all our experience we have found that to issue, as the willow stands near the water and sends out its roots in that direction. This will vary with different natures, but this is the place where a wise man will dig his cellar.

Thoreau finds solitude wholesome and society, even with the best, to be wearisome and dissipating. "I love to be alone," he writes, "I never found the companion that was so companionable as solitude." Society is commonly too superficial. Mostly we have nothing of value to share. Perhaps if we spent more time with our thoughts we have something worth communicating.

Thoreau compares his own solitude with that of nature, including that of the loon, the sun, and Walden Pond itself. He alludes to visits he has had from the spirits of Pan, the Greek god of all the inhabitants of the countryside, and Mother Nature, in communion with which he feels part and parcel of the earth and the elemental forces of nature: "Shall I not have intelligence with the earth? Am I not partly leaves and vegetable mould myself?"

In another of many references to the morning, which for Thoreau is always a metaphor for spiritual awakening, he says that "the pill which will keep us well, serene, contented" is nothing other than "a draught of undiluted morning air." Solitude seems to be a necessary condition for the imbibing of this particular elixir.

Chapter Summary of "Visitors"

This chapter is paired with the previous one in treating the dichotomy of solitude and society. Thoreau is actually seeking a balance between the needs and demands of both. Contrary to what readers might conclude from the chapter on solitude, Thoreau says that he loves society "as much as most," and that he is "naturally no hermit." He had three chairs in his house, he writes: "one for solitude, two for friendship, three for society." He suggests by this that a balanced life entails the use, by turns, of all three.

The fact is, Thoreau had many visitors to his cabin, curious, no doubt, about his experiment in simple living and the conditions of his existence at Walden Pond. On at least one occasion he seems to have had twenty-five or thirty at the same time. Yet, for all the numbers in such a confined space, he is aware of the distance that people naturally put between themselves. Indeed, he feels that there needs to be a "considerable neutral ground" in even the best of relationships. Furthermore, the discussion of expansive thoughts requires ample room. As Thoreau himself puts it: "if we speak reservedly and thoughtfully, we want to be farther apart."

He does feel that he met some of his visitors under more favorable circumstances at Walden Pond than elsewhere, partly, no doubt, because of the natural surroundings, but also because, at that distance from town, fewer came to see him on trivial business.

⑥

For a full day and two nights I have been alone . . . And it seemed to me, separated from my own species, that I was nearer to others . . . I felt a kind of impersonal kinship with them and a joy in that kinship. Beauty of earth and sea and air meant more to me. I was in harmony with it, melted into the universe, lost in it, as one is lost in a canticle of praise, swelling from an unknown crowd in a cathedral . . . .

Yes, I felt closer to my fellow men too, even in my solitude. For it is not physical solitude that actually separates one from other men, not physical isolation, but spiritual isolation. It is not the desert island nor the stony wilderness that cuts you from the people you love. It is the wilderness in the mind, the desert wastes in the heart through which one wanders lost and a stranger. When one is a stranger to oneself then one is estranged from others, too. If one is out of touch with oneself, then one cannot touch others. How often in a large city, shaking hands with my friends, I have felt the wilderness stretching between us. Both of us were wandering in arid wastes, having lost the springs that nourished us—or having found them dry. Only when one is connected to one's own core is one connected to others . . . And for me, the core, the inner spring can best be refound through solitude.

—Anne Morrow Lindbergh, *Gift from the Sea*

Questions for Discussion

- Thoreau relished the solitude he encountered at Walden Pond. How do you find solitude in your life? Have you ever experienced sustained periods of it? What did that feel like?

- Thoreau says that through solitude he felt in communion with the earth and the forces of nature. Have you had such an experience yourself? Can you describe it?

- There are those who argue that Thoreau is unrealistic because his cultivation of the "eternal moments" precluded human relations and thus he isn't a reliable guru for our times. In their view Thoreau wished to be an island to himself. Do you agree or disagree? Is this your understanding of Thoreau's message?

- Buddhist priest Thich Nhat Hanh says, "We are so busy we hardly have time to look at the people we love, even in our own household, and to look at ourselves. Society is organized in a way that even when we have some leisure time, we don't know how to use it to get back in touch with ourselves. . . . We are not

used to being with ourselves, and we act as if we don't like ourselves and are trying to escape from ourselves." Do you agree?
How do you use your leisure time? How do you get back in
touch with yourself?

- Like Thoreau, Ralph Waldo Emerson was also concerned with
  striking a balance between solitude and society. In his essay
  on "Society and Solitude," Emerson writes the following: "Here
  again, as so often, nature delights to put us between extreme
  antagonisms, and our safety is in the skill with which we keep
  the diagonal line. Solitude is impractical and society fatal. We
  must keep our head in the one and our hands in the other. The
  conditions are met, if we keep our independence, yet do not
  lose our sympathy. These wonderful horses need to be driven
  by fine hands. We require such a solitude as shall hold us to its
  revelations when we are in the street and in palaces." Does this
  make sense to you? How do you strike such a balance in your
  own life?

- In *Gift from the Sea*, Anne Morrow Lindbergh makes the following comment: "If one sets aside time for a business engagement,
  a trip to the hairdresser, a social engagement, or a shopping
  expedition, that time is accepted as inviolable. But if one says: I
  cannot come because that is my hour to be alone, one is considered rude, egotistical or strange. What a commentary on our
  civilization, when being alone is considered suspect; when one
  has to apologize for it, make excuses, hide the fact that one
  practices it—like a secret vice!" Do you feel guilty for seeking
  solitude? Do you give up time for yourself because of other
  obligations?

Additional Resources

Buchholz, Ester Schaler, *The Call of Solitude: Alonetime in a World of
Attachment,* Simon and Schuster, 1997.

Campbell, Eileen, ed., *Silence and Solitude: Inspirations for Meditation
and Spiritual Growth,* HarperCollins, 1994.

Emerson, Ralph Waldo, *Society and Solitude,* Houghton Mifflin, 1904.

Lindbergh, Anne Morrow, *Gift from the Sea*, Pantheon, 1955.

Salwak, Dale, ed., *The Wonders of Solitude*, New World Library, 1995.

Sarton, May, *Journal of a Solitude,* Norton, 1973.

Storr, Anthony, *Solitude: A Return to the Self*, Ballentine, 1988.

⑥

"I love the wild not less than the good."

READING "HIGHER LAWS"

⑥

If the day and the night are such that you greet them with joy, and life emits a fragrance like flowers and sweet-scented herbs, is more elastic, more starry, more immortal—that is your success. All nature is your congratulation, and you have cause momentarily to bless yourself. The greatest gains and values are farthest from being appreciated. We easily come to doubt if they exist. We soon forget them. They are the highest reality. Perhaps the facts most astounding and most real are never communicated by man to man. The true harvest of my daily life is somewhat as intangible and indescribable as the tints of morning or evening. It is a little stardust caught, a segment of the rainbow which I have clutched. —HDT

Chapter Summary

The concept of "higher laws" was central to Transcendentalist thought. It represented the ideal order of things, as opposed to the material or worldly order. It stood as a goal of the spiritual life to live according to these laws, and was a criterion by which human actions were judged. It was on the basis of the higher law, for example, that Thoreau, Theodore Parker and other Transcendentalists condemned the proslavery laws passed by Congress. This chapter is Thoreau at his most religious, although his beliefs are quite unconventional by Christian standards.

He begins with the rather shocking statement that he was once tempted to eat a woodchuck raw, not because he was hungry, but because he wished to consume the wildness that the animal represented. Indeed, he confesses, "I found in myself, and still find, an instinct toward a higher, or, as it is named, spiritual life, as do most men, and another toward a primitive rank and savage one, and I reverence them both. I love the wild not less than the good." Thoreau wished to be faithful both to nature, which is essentially wild, and to the higher, spiritual life. This is not surprising, since, for Thoreau, the way to the spiritual life is through the natural world.

Those who spend time in the fields and woods, such as hunters, fishermen, woodchoppers and the like, have the advantage that their work brings them in proximity to Nature, and, therefore, closer to the realm of the spirit. However, those who would aspire to a higher life must cease to kill. If the hunter or fisherman has "the seeds of the better life in him," he soon "leaves the gun and fish-pole behind."

Thoreau used to fish himself till he lost his self-respect in doing so. Not only did he cease to fish, but he attempted to become a vegetarian. He even swore off coffee and tea, because they did not agree with his "imagination." In his abstinence from meat and stimulating drinks, Thoreau pursued an asceticism which he hoped would transform him from a "grosser," form of existence into a more spiritual one.

Like Emerson and other Transcendentalists, Thoreau believed that one came into the world with his or her own genius, a sort of guiding light or guardian angel. This is why he was so confident that in following the promptings of one's genius, one was inevitably led along the path to the higher life. Thoreau puts it this way:

> If one listens to the faintest but constant suggestions of his genius, which are certainly true, he sees not to what extremes, or even in-

sanity, it may lead him; and yet that way, as he grows more resolute and faithful, his road lies. . . . No man ever followed his genius till it misled him. Though the result were bodily weakness, yet perhaps no one can say that the consequences were to be regretted, for these were a life in conformity to higher principles.

He goes on to describe the epiphany that awaits those who persist in pursuing their genius: "If the day and the night are such that you greet them with joy, and life emits a fragrance like flowers and sweet-scented herbs, is more elastic, more starry, more immortal—that is your success. All nature is your congratulation, and you have cause momentarily to bless yourself."

So contrary to ordinary, every-day consciousness is this experience that it is easily overlooked and seldom appreciated. It is easily doubted and soon forgotten. And yet it represents the highest reality. Ironically, what is most important is also the hardest to express. "The true harvest of my daily life," he says, "is somewhat as intangible and indescribable as the tints of morning or evening. It is a little star-dust caught, a segment of the rainbow which I have clutched."

Still, Thoreau is honest about his own limitations. He admits to eating "a fried rat with good relish" on occasion. He practices sobriety, but does not consider himself a thoroughgoing ascetic. More important than one's appetite for meat and drink is the mental attitude that accompanies it. "Our whole life," he says, "is startlingly moral. There is never an instant's truce between virtue and vice. Goodness is the only investment that never fails." And therefore it matters what our intentions are.

Always, we are conscious of the animal in us, "which awakens in proportion as our higher nature slumbers." It cannot wholly be expelled. "Yet the spirit can for the time pervade and control every member and function of the body," he says, "and transmute what in form is the grossest sensuality into purity and devotion." In the discussion of chastity that follows Thoreau lapses into a dualism of spirit and body, arguing that only through "cleanliness" can sensuality be overcome. In a reference to Paul's Letter to the Corinthians, Thoreau insists that "Every man is the builder of a temple, called his body, to the god he worships, after a style purely his own, nor can he get off by hammering marble instead."

Thoreau closes the chapter with a fable about John Farmer. Undoubtedly, he means John the Farmer, that is to say, everyman, rather a real individual. This person has worked hard all day, his mind still absorbed in his labors. Bathing, he takes his ease and begins to think of more intellectual matters. Soon he becomes aware of the sound of a flute, the music of which begins to play in his head and makes his thoughts seem less important that they were.

It is apparent that the notes of the flute come to him from "a different sphere from that he worked in, and suggested work for certain faculties which slumbered in him." The everyday realities of his life—where he lived and what he did for a living—ceased to matter so much. A voice spoke to him, saying, "Why do you stay here and live this mean and moiling life, when a glorious existence is possible for you? Those same stars twinkle over other fields than these."

But how was he to depart from his customary way of life and take up residence in this new, more spiritual realm? "All that he could think of was to practice some new austerity," Thoreau says, "to let his mind descend into his body and redeem it, and treat himself with ever-increasing respect." This is a critical question for us as well.

⑥

The soul of each of us is given a unique daimon before we are born, and it has selected an image or pattern that we live on earth. This soul-companion, the daimon, guides us here; in the process of arrival, however, we forget all that took place and believe we come empty into this world. The daimon remembers what is in your image and belong to yor pattern, and therefore your daimon is the carrier of your destiny. . . .

The myth leads also to practical moves. . . . (a) Recognize the call as a prime fact of human existence; (b) align life with it; (c) find the common sense to realize that accidents, including the heartache and the natural shocks the flesh is heir to, belong to the pattern of the image, are necessary to it, and help fulfill it.

A calling may be postponed, avoided, intermittently missed. It may also possess you completely. Whatever; eventually it will out. It makes its claim. The daimon does not go away.

—James Hillman,
The Soul's Code: in Search of Character and Calling

Questions for Discussion

- Thoreau says he "loves the wild not less than the good." What do you think he means by this? What does the wild mean to you? Does the word disturb you in any way?

- Many religions, including Christianity and Hinduism, have taught that to live the spiritual life means renouncing the body and the natural, material world. Thoreau argues that the higher life is found through Nature, and therefore he reverences them both. What is your view?

- Thoreau was a part-time vegetarian. What is your view of vegetarianism? Are you vegetarian? Why or why not?

- Thoreau avoided smoking and drinking (including wine, tea and coffee) as well as meat on the view that it did not agree with his "imagination." What do you suppose he means by this? He considered his body a temple which he did not wish to defile. What is your view of such wholesale "temperance"? He seemed to feel that a certain amount of asceticism was necessary to achieve a spiritual life. What do you think? Do you practice any form of asceticism?

- For the Transcendentalists, genius was not talent, but an inner spiritual guide which was trustworthy and, if followed, was certain to lead one to a successful and fulfilled life. James Hillman, in *The Soul's Code*, seems to agree. What do you say? What would it mean to you to follow the promptings of your genius? When was the last time you heard from your genius? What did you do? Have you ever experienced an epiphany such as awaits those who follow their genius?

- Thoreau describes "the true harvest" of his daily life as something "as intangible and indescribable as the tints of morning or evening. It is a little star-dust caught, a segment of the rainbow which I have clutched." What is "the true harvest" of your daily life?

- Thoreau is honest about his own limitations. How would you describe yours (assuming you have any)?

- Thoreau insists that "our whole life is startlingly moral. There is never an instant's truce between virtue and vice." Do you agree? What does it mean to live in a moral universe?

- Does the fable of John Farmer make any sense to you? Have you ever heard similar flute music summoning you to a higher life? How do you reconcile in your own life the everyday realities of job and home with the call to a more spiritual form of existence? What would such change require of you?

Additional Resources

Hillman, James, *The Soul's Code: in Search of Character and Calling,* Random House, 1996.

Huxley, Aldous, *The Perennial Philosophy*, Harper, 1944.

Moore, Thomas, *The Re-Enchantment of Everyday Life*, Harper, 1996.

HOW THEN SHALL WE LIVE?

(b)

"Only that day dawns to which we are awake. There is more day to dawn. The sun is but a morning star."

READING "CONCLUSION"

(b)

I learned this, at least, by my experiment: that if one advances confidently in the direction of his dreams, and endeavors to live the life which he has imagined, he will meet with a success unexpected in common hours. He will put some things behind, will pass an invisible boundary; new, universal, and more liberal laws will begin to establish themselves around and within his; or the old laws be expanded, and interpreted in his favor in a more liberal sense, and he will live with the license of a higher order of beings. In proportion as he simplifies his life, the laws of the universe will appear less complex, and solitude will not be solitude, nor poverty poverty, nor weakness weakness. If you have built castles in the air, your work need not be lost; that is where they should be. Now put the foundations under them. —HDT

Thoreau was a notorious stay-at-home. Although he was steeped in the literature of travel and exploration, he never ventured far from his birthplace. He made several excursions to Quebec, the Maine woods and Cape Cod. For a brief period he tutored Emerson's nephews on Staten Island, and, late in his life, he made a trip to Minnesota for his health. For the most part, however, he was content to bloom where he was planted. As he preferred to put it, "I have travelled a good deal in Concord."

In this chapter Thoreau uses metaphors of travel and exploration to suggest that we should view our own lives as an adventure or a quest, and that the undiscovered territory we seek is not so much elsewhere, in some remote corner of the globe, but is actually within ourselves. He begins, however, with a little indirection. He says that what we see around us is not all that there is. The tendency is to settle down and set bounds to our life and to act as though our fate has been decided. But, he declares, "The universe is wider than our views of it."

We should look beyond our current situation, like curious passengers at the railing of their ship, and not like the sailors who merely toil at their tasks, missing out on the view. Pursuing the metaphor of travel further, Thoreau asserts that it is not really the game in Africa we seek; the real quarry is ourselves. Quoting a bit of poetry, he declares:

> Direct your eye right inward, and you'll find
> A thousand regions in your mind
> Yet undiscovered. Travel them, and be
> Expert in home-cosmography

In Thoreau's day the interior of Africa was as yet undiscovered. Is not our own interior also mystery, he asks? And is it really the source of the Nile that we are looking for, or rather the headwaters of our spiritual life? In a reference to other explorers, he says, "Be rather the Mungo Park, the Lewis and Clark and Frobisher of your own streams and oceans; explore your own higher latitudes. . . . Nay, be a Columbus to whole new continents and worlds within you, opening new channels, not of trade, but of thought." Each of us commands a realm within beside which the empire of the Czar pales in comparison. Continuing in this vein, he sees in these elaborate exploring expeditions

> . . . an indirect recognition of the fact that there are continents and seas in the moral world to which every man is an isthmus or an inlet, yet unexplored by him, but that it is easier to sail many thousand miles through cold and storm and cannibals, in a government ship, with five hundred men and boys to assist one, than it is to explore the private sea, the Atlantic and Pacific Ocean of one's being alone.

If you would fancy yourself well-travelled, he says, if you would be an explorer, then "obey the precept of the old philosopher, and Explore thyself. Herein are demanded the eye and the nerve."

Thoreau left the woods feeling that he had "several more lives to live, and could not spare any more time for that one." His life there had become routine. How predictable were the "ruts of tradition and conformity!" He needed a change. As he put it: "I did not wish to take a cabin passage, but rather to go before the mast and on the deck of the world, for there I could best see the moonlight amid the mountains. I do not wish to go below now." However, he did learn by his experiment that "if one advances confidently in the direction of his dreams, and endeavors to live the life which he has imagined, he will meet with a success unexpected in common hours." Those who are able to "put some things behind" will discover a sense of personal freedom and power. To the extent that we are able to simplify our lives, as Thoreau did at Walden Pond, "the laws of the universe will appear less complex, and solitude will not be solitude, nor poverty poverty, nor weakness weakness."

Thoreau is aware that others might think his philosophy and lifestyle extreme, but feels that he must exaggerate to some extent in order get his point across. Indeed, he fears he's not "extra-vagant" enough, using the word in the sense of wandering beyond the "narrow limits" of common experience. "I desire to speak somewhere *without* bounds," he writes; "like a man in a waking moment to men in their waking moments; for I am convinced that I cannot exaggerate enough even to lay the foundation of a true expression." Sometimes one must shout in order to be heard.

61

The problem is, we settle for too little. We prize our dullest perceptions as common sense when, in fact, what passes for common sense is really the sense of people who are asleep. We wouldn't recognize a wise person if we saw one. Some believe that we are intellectually inferior to our ancestors and let it go at that. Shouldn't we rather be the most intelligent persons we can possibly be? We seem so desperate to succeed and in such desperate enterprises. Instead, we should do what is right for us. As Thoreau says in a well-known passage: "If a man does not keep pace with his companions, perhaps it is because he hears a different drummer. Let him step to the music which he hears, however measured or far away." We should not settle for anything less than the truth.

Thoreau tells a fable of an artist in the city of Kouroo who sought perfection in his art. He thought that time was a factor only in relation to an imperfect work, whereas to achieve perfection would put him beyond time's reach. He proceeded to carve a staff, and worked at it with such concentration and attention to detail that, without realizing it, he entered the realm of the eternal now. While he was engaged with his task whole eons of time passed, but he remained perennially young. In making the staff he had created a new world "with full and fair proportions; in which, though the old cities and dynasties had passed away, fairer and more glorious ones had taken their places."

Thoreau's advice is to love your life, no matter how poor it seems; poverty is only relative anyway. In fact, poverty, freely chosen, allows us to live the most independent lives of any. In a passage reminiscent of what Jesus said about the lilies of the field, Thoreau admonishes us to

> Cultivate poverty like a garden herb, like sage. Do not trouble yourself much to get new things, whether clothes or friends. Turn the old; return to them. Things do not change; we change. Sell your clothes and keep your thoughts. God will see that you do not want society.

We may not be able to afford some things, but poverty has the advantage at least that we are compelled to deal with the material that yields the most—our own selves. "It is life near the bone where it is sweetest." Wealth can purchase superfluities only. "Money," he says, "is not required to purchase one necessary of the soul."

Thoreau is not interested in hearing about the lifestyles of the rich and famous. Talk of celebrities is trivial: "a goose is still a goose, dress it as you will." Rather than marching "in procession with pomp and parade," he would "walk even with the Builder of the universe." He wishes only "to weigh, to settle, to gravitate toward that which most strongly and rightfully attracts" him; to accept life as it is; "to travel the only path that I can, and that on which no power can resist me." He seeks a solid bottom on which to stand, and not "the bogs and quicksand of society." He will not be satisfied with halfway measures. Even the smallest details in life should matter:

> Drive a nail home and clinch it so faithfully that you can wake up in the night and think of your work with satisfaction—a work at which you would not be ashamed to invoke the Muse. So will help you God, and so only. Every nail driven should be as another rivet in the machine of the universe, you carrying on the work.

We underestimate ourselves. We have barely scratched the surface of the globe on which we live. "Most have not delved six feet beneath the surface nor leaped as many above it." We do not know where we are. Half the time we are sound asleep. "There is an incessant influx of novelty into the world," Thoreau reflects, "and yet we tolerate incredible dullness." He is hopeful that our lives will someday rise like the water in a river, and flood our parched uplands. He cites the story of a bug which came out of a table that had stood in a farmer's home for sixty years, hatched from an egg deposited in the living tree many years earlier. The incident teaches an extraordinary lesson:

> Who does not feel his faith in a resurrection and immortality strengthened by hearing of this? Who knows what beautiful and winged life, whose egg has been buried for ages under many concentric layers of woodenness in the dead dry life of society, deposited at first in the alburnum of the green and living tree, which has been gradually converted into the semblance of a well-seasoned tomb—heard perchance gnawing out now for years by the astonished family of man, as they sat round the festive board—may unexpectedly come forth from amidst society's most trivial and handselled furniture, to enjoy its perfect summer life at last!

63

Not everyone will hear this message; only those who are prepared to listen. As Thoreau says in the memorable closing lines of *Walden*: "Only that day dawns to which we are awake. There is more day to dawn. The sun is but a morning star."

⑥

Thoreau called Americans away from their overabsorption with economic life, from their self-subjugation to a life of toil. Unlike earlier advocates of simple living, he was not calling people to religion or to civic engagement; rather he was calling us as individuals to find our own true nature, to define ourselves at a higher level of experience. He called for simple living in order to enable the life of the mind, of art, literature, poetry, philosophy, and an almost reverential engagement with Nature.
— Jerome M. Segal, *Graceful Simplicity:*
Toward a Philosophy and Politics of Simple Living

Questions for Discussion

- When was the last time you travelled? What was the experience of travelling like? Do you approach life like curious passengers at the railing of their ship, or like the sailors who merely toil at their tasks without looking up?

- Thoreau insists that it is our own interior, not the interior of Africa that we should seek. Do you agree? What have you done to explore your own higher latitudes?

- Have you ever felt that you had more lives to live? Did you make any changes in your life as a result? How do you keep your life from becoming routine?

- Thoreau feels that if we advance confidently in the direction of our dreams we will meet a success unexpected in common hours. What do you think? Has this ever been true for you?

- Have you done anything to simplify your own life? What did you do? What did you discover about yourself as a result?

- What is the meaning, for you, of Thoreau's fable about the artist of Kouroo? Have you ever had a similar experience?

- Thoreau asserts that "money is not required to buy one necessary of the soul." Do you agree? What would you say are the necessaries of the soul?

- How do you avoid what seems trivial and superficial in the world around you? How do you know what "most strongly and rightfully" attracts you? What is a solid bottom for you?

- In spite of his criticism of society—which can be quite caustic at times—Thoreau is no pessimist. As we see in the tale of the bug in the table, he has faith in resurrection, in the possibility of new life. Do you? What evidence of hope do you see?

Additional Resources

Phil Cousineau, *The Art of Pilgrimage: The Seeker's Guide to Making Travel Sacred,* Conari Press, 1998.

Jerome M. Segal, *Graceful Simplicity: Toward a Philosophy and Politics of Simple Living,* Henry Holt, 1999.

Philip Zaleski and Paul Kaufman, *Gifts of the Spirit: Living the Wisdom of the Great Religious Traditions,* HarperCollins, 1998.

1817   Born July 12 in Concord, MA, "the most estimable
        place in all the world, and in the very nick of time,
        too." The third of four children. Family attends the
        Unitarian church.

1833-37 Attends Harvard College. Delivers commencement
        speech: "The order of things should be somewhat re-
        versed; the seventh should be man's day of toil, wherein
        to earn his living by the sweat of his brow; and the
        other six his Sabbath of the affections and the soul—in
        which to range this widespread garden, and drink in
        the soft influences and sublime revelations of Nature."

1837   Teaches for a few weeks in the Concord public school.
        Quits because he refuses to whip students. Becomes a
        member of the Transcendentalist "club." Begins Jour-
        nal at the Emerson's urging.

1838   Begins teaching at Concord Academy. First lecture at
        Concord Lyceum. First excursion to Maine.

1839   Meets Ellen Sewell. Excursion on Concord and Merri-
        mack Rivers with brother John.

1840   First essays and poems published in the Dial magazine,
        a Transcendentalist publication edited by Margaret
        Fuller and Ralph Waldo Emerson. Proposes to Ellen
        Sewell, but her father refuses to allow the marriage.

1841	Closes school and moves into the Emerson, where he lives for two years.
1842	Brother John dies of lockjaw. Meets Hawthorne. "Natural History of Massachusetts" published in Dial.
1843	Tutors the children of Emerson's brother, William, on Staten Island for six months. Meets Horace Greeley.
1845	Moves to cabin built on Emerson's property at Walden Pond on July 4. "I went to the woods because I wished to live deliberately, to front only the essential facts of life, and see if I could not learn what it had to teach, and not, when I came to die, discover that I had not lived."
1846	Arrested for non-payment of poll tax in protest of slavery; spends one night in jail. Second trip to Maine.
1847	Leaves Walden Pond. "I left the woods for as good a reason as I went there. Perhaps it seemed to me that I had several more lives to live, and could not spend any more time for that one." Moves in with the Emersons again for 10 months while RWE travels in Europe.
1848	Delivers lecture on "Resistance to Civil Government" (posthumously known as "Civil Disobedience"). "Ktaadn and the Maine Woods" serialized.
1849	Publishes first book, *A Week on the Concord and Merrimack Rivers*. First trip to Cape Cod. Sister Helen dies of tuberculosis.
1850	Death of Margaret Fuller; Thoreau goes to Fire Island, NY, to search for remains. Trip to Canada.
1851	Fugitive Slave Act passed. Becomes involved in Underground Railroad.
1854	*Walden* published. Lectures on "Slavery in Massachusetts."
1855	"Cape Cod" serialized.

1856   Meets Walt Whitman in Brooklyn: "He is apparently
        the greatest democrat the world has seen."

1857   Trips to Cape Cod again, and to Maine. John Brown
        visits Concord. Brown has much support among the
        Transcendentalists.

1859   Father dies. Delivers defiant address, "A Plea for Cap-
        tain John Brown."

1860   Writes "Last Days of John Brown." Camping trip leads
        to fatal illness.

1861   Trip to Minnesota for health reasons. Makes last visit
        to Walden Pond. Beginning of Civil War.

1862   Dies of tuberculosis on May 6 in Concord. Asked on
        his death bed if he could see the "other side," Thoreau
        replies: "One world at a time." *Maine Woods, Cape
        Cod*, "Life Without Principle" and "Walking"
        published posthumously.